GROUPS TO GO

Small Groups For Counselors On The Go

14 Ready-To-Use Small-Group Counseling Plans
For Grades K-3

ACADEMIC IMPROVEMENT
Listening: A Study Skill
Concentration: A Study Skill
Another Year In The Same Grade
Time Management
Study Skills—Work Habits
Making The Decision To Learn

BEHAVIOR
Anger
Facing Reality
Attention Seeking
Controlling Anger

UNDERSTANDING SELF AND OTHERS
Self-Esteem
Shy Or Withdrawn Students
Self-Confidence
Friendship

Written By
Arden Martenz

Illustrated By Brian Dumm

GROUPS TO GO: SMALL GROUPS FOR COUNSELORS ON THE GO/K-3

10-DIGIT ISBN: 1-57543-148-3 13-DIGIT ISBN: 978-1-57543-148-2

REPRINTED 2008

Published by mar*co products, inc.
1443 Old York Road
Warminster, PA 18974
1-800-448-2197
www.marcoproducts.com

PRINTED IN THE U.S.A.

Sherolyn Botthing
TCA Conference
Nov 2011

TABLE OF CONTENTS

WELCOME TO
GROUPS TO GO

Small-group counseling is the backbone of elementary counseling. It is the major service provided by a counselor that no one else in the school is trained to do. I once attended a seminar where the speaker said, "Problems that originate in groups, need to be addressed and solved in groups." Most problems facing young children are rooted in one group or another—peer groups or family groups. Hence, the importance of small-group counseling.

Groups To Go for kindergarten through third grade targets the three topics most necessary to address at the early elementary level—academic improvement, behavior, and understanding self and others. You will find four or more groups within each of these topics, and each emphasizes a different approach to the topic.

The book was designed in this manner because young children often need more than one small-group experience on a topic. For example, a child who is having difficulty with listening skills may also need reinforcement of concentration and study skills.

Time is always a factor during the school day. There is always more to do than time allows. Therefore, if students are going to be taken from their classrooms the amount of time missed has to be minimal. The sessions in *Groups To Go* are scheduled to be completed in 30 to 40 minutes. Small-group counseling is a child's opportunity for expression and reflection. If at first glance the sessions seem to be short, once involved in discussion the time will pass quickly and productively.

The selected groups in *Groups To Go* have been used with children. Most have been adapted from issues of *PIC* (*Practical Ideas For Counselors*), a counselor newsletter which was written by Mar∗co staff and contributing counselors. Unless otherwise specified, the groups in this book were written and conducted in the school system by counselors who were members of Mar∗co's staff. They have been written to be as user-friendly as possible and include the techniques that proved most successful. However, each school is different. So is every child. Although each session includes step-by-step directions, you may find that you need to make adaptations to fit your particular situation. If necessary, adjust the sessions to give your students the best experience possible.

Although *Groups To Go* has been created to make your small group counseling program easy to initiate and continue, it must be remembered that...

Nobody ever said group counseling was easy...

Counselors can find group counseling a rewarding or frustrating experience. If group members change their behavior, counselors feel a tremendous sense of satisfaction and pride. But when one member behaves in a way that prevents the group from functioning, the group itself lacks cohesion. The leader is not in control, and the experience becomes one many counselors do not want to repeat. To prevent this from happening, here are 10 tips on what to do when problems arise.

What can you do when one member constantly disrupts the group?

Mary will not stop interrupting when another group member is talking. She is so determined to talk about her concerns that her talking dominates each group session.

Group counseling may not be the best way to work with this type of student. Carefully examine Mary's problem and her needs and ask yourself if her needs are so great that it is unreasonable to expect her to share counseling time with other students. If the answer to the question is "yes," Mary would probably benefit more from individual counseling. It is sometimes better for this type of student to learn to relate to one person before attempting to relate to several people. Through individual counseling, the counselor can help Mary with her problem while helping her learn to function in a group. As Mary makes progress, she may spend part of her counseling time with the group and part in individual sessions. Make sure that Mary understands the ultimate goal is for her to function as a member of a group.

Suppose after examining the problem carefully, the counselor feels Mary would benefit from group counseling. If that is the case, group consequences must be established for students who interrupt. An example of an appropriate consequence is that anyone who interrupts someone else would not be allowed to speak for the rest of the session. The consequence could be defined so that the interrupting student not only did not speak, but sat apart from the group and observed for the rest of the session. A counselor who uses this technique should ask the interrupting student to remain for a few minutes after the group has left so the two of them can discuss why the student was not part of the group and what the student must do to remain part of the group during subsequent sessions.

What can you do when one group member is always "picked on"?

According to the group, Mike is always doing something wrong. If he says something, the others criticize him. If he does something in class, the group reports it at the counseling session. No matter what happens in the group, it seems Mike is always to blame.

One group member will occasionally be singled out as a "troublemaker." This is usually an unpopular student. Counselors may approach the problem in two ways.

First, determine whether the blame is justified. If it is, the counselor may conduct some group sessions that key in on individual students' problems rather than on a group problem. Place a chair so it faces the group members. Then tell the group that for the next few sessions, their task will be to help group members change their behavior. They can do this by being honest and telling the student sitting in the chair what behavior they think he/she should change. The student sitting in the chair may not respond in any way while group members are talking. Begin by selecting any group member, except the one who is always blamed, to sit in the chair. Explain that each student will tell the person in the chair something he/she believes would help him/her be better liked. Then have each student say something to the student sitting in the chair. When each group member has had a turn, ask the student sitting in the chair to select one of the ideas expressed and make that change before the next session. Continue the exercise, using other group members and including the student who is always blamed. At the next session, have the group members report on how they performed their tasks. Encourage all the students to continue behaving positively. For students for whom it would be helpful, suggest making changes other than those mentioned previously.

If the counselor decides the blaming is not justified, the group rule that no one may put another student down should be enforced and consequences should be established for those who break the rule. If the situation is critical, the counselor may decide to hold a session that does not include the harassed student in order to discuss what is going on and what can put a stop to this group behavior.

What can you do when a group member doesn't participate?

David never has anything to contribute to group discussions. He sits quietly and apparently listens to what others say, but never volunteers. When asked his opinion, he says, "I don't know."

Shy students, students who have difficulty expressing their thoughts, or students who are insecure in groups often sit quietly and let others do all the talking. This can frustrate the counselor who feels unable to reach these group members.

One way to involve this type of student is to vary group activities. It is the counselor's responsibility to find ways to involve each group member, and if oral discussions do not meet everyone's needs, a different approach should be taken. Create an art activity that will fit into the group's purpose. When everyone has finished, have all the students share their drawings. This will give the non-verbal student like David something concrete to talk about. If he still has difficulty expressing himself, the counselor should sit near him and help him begin the task. If David still cannot participate, the counselor should evaluate whether group counseling is the best way to work with him. A few individual counseling sessions may help the student feel more secure. Then he can return to the group.

What can you do if a group member violates confidentiality?

Clarissa knew one of the group rules was that she could discuss anything she talked about, but nothing that other group members talked about. After a discussion about family life, Clarissa went back to the classroom and told her best friend about the troubles another group member was having at home.

In certain groups, the essential nature of confidentiality must be emphasized. It may be necessary to remind students before each session begins and again at the end of each session how critical this issue is. Depending upon the age of the students, it also may be necessary to give examples of what can happen when a group member violates confidentiality. Group members must realize that violating confidentiality can embarrass or hurt fellow group members and make them distrustful. Because confidentiality is important, the leader should establish consequences that will occur if confidentiality is violated. A logical consequence would be that Clarissa would no longer be a member of the group. Explain the reason for this consequence by telling the students that when personal things are revealed outside the group, it is difficult to restore the group's trust level. It is even more difficult to do this if the outspoken student is still a member of the group. To preserve the group, in other words, it is necessary to eliminate the student who could destroy it.

The counselor could be in a difficult situation if Clarissa denied that she violated confidentiality. If this happens, the counselor must speak with Clarissa privately. Before this individual session, it is important for the counselor to make every effort to determine whether the incident actually happened the way it was reported.

What can you do when the group's composition prevents progress?

Mr. Adams, the school counselor, works with a group of boys who have behavior problems. They are all from the same class and have known each other for a number of years. Whenever the group is in session, Mr. Adams spends a great deal of time telling the boys to correct their behavior so the session can continue.

There are times when group composition prevents progress. No matter what the counselor tries, the group is just not cohesive. This can happen when the group members know each other very well or lack leadership strength. One way to prevent this problem is to scrutinize each student before setting up the group. Check to see whether potential group members play with each other at recess, participate in the same outside activities, have been in classes together, or live in the same neighborhood. If two or more of these conditions exist, it is probably not a good idea to put these students in the same group.

If the problem arises after the group is formed, try to add new members and form two groups. This allows the counselor to select students who have not had much contact with the other members. If the group cannot be split, the counselor may have to either terminate the group or complete the contracted number of sessions with the understanding that no significant changes will occur.

What can you do if group members are not changing their behavior?

Each week, the counselor talks with the group about ways to make friends. The students verbalize what they must do and say they will try to do better when they return to their classes. When the counselor checks with the teachers, she learns that the students are not doing any better.

Counselors sometimes must be direct when discussing expectations for behavior change. Young students need specific, concrete directions to follow. Identify the expected behavior change, decide upon a method for making the change, and regularly evaluate the students' progress. Each student must know exactly what change he/she needs to make. Once the change is identified, the counselor should help the student outline a step-by-step procedure for making the change. One method of evaluation is to provide the classroom teacher with a simple form on which to indicate whether the contracted behavior took place during the specified time. A sample form would be:

Louise Parker will not bother any students at the water fountain during the week of ***Oct. 5***.

Signed ***Louise Parker***

Louise did/did not fulfill the behavior contract.

Signed ***Mrs. Spencer***

What do you do when the group is not cohesive?

Mrs. Zee had planned the group session carefully. Moments after the session started, the students began to whisper, wiggle, and giggle. As soon as one student started to misbehave, the rest followed suit. Mrs. Zee had to continually remind them to settle down and think about what they were supposed to be doing.

Know your group members. Counselors who know their group members and how they behave in class will be better able to plan group sessions. A brief conference with the classroom teacher before group sessions begin will provide this information.

A 30-minute discussion period is as much of an eternity for a group of restless students as a 30-minute classroom work period. If the classroom teacher discussed this problem with the counselor, the counselor would suggest that the teacher vary the activities. The counselor should do the same. Restless students need variety. Divide the counseling session into two or three activities related to the group's purpose. If you do, students will be better able to pay attention and learn what is expected of them.

What can you do when you lose control?

Each session is a hassle. The group members enter the room and refuse to do what the counselor has planned. Sometimes the students convince the counselor to change his/her plans and let them talk about what they want to talk about. Sometimes they make fun of what they are to do by telling the counselor the activity is for babies. They sabotage the group each week, and the counselor feels completely at their mercy.

Should this group *be* a group? Some students referred for group counseling truly do not want to be members of a counseling group. If their desire to get out is strong enough, they will do almost anything to get their wish. Admit defeat. By honestly admitting to the students that their lack of cooperation is defeating the group's purpose, you will not be telling them anything they do not already know. You will only be letting them know you are aware of the situation. Students who *want* control respond when *given* control. So the counselor must allow the students to have a say in making and implementing decisions that affect the group.

Begin by asking if the group members want the sessions to continue. If they do not, disband the group and work with the students individually or through the classroom teacher. If the students want to continue, tell them that everyone must work together to fulfill the group's purpose. Set group goals, rules, and consequences based on insight and input from group members. By allowing the students to decide whether to participate in the group, you have given them some control over its continuance or termination. By allowing the students to help set the goals, rules, and consequences, you have given them some control over the group's administration. Students who participate in setting goals, rules, and consequences feel they have a part in the group's functioning and will respond in a more positive way. If some students want to leave and others want to stay, keep those who want to be involved and work with them on setting the group standards. Let the others leave. Don't make continuance or termination of the group dependent upon a majority vote. That eliminates the individual control that is important to each student.

What can you do when group members don't trust the leader?

The counselor has coffee with the classroom teachers every day. They meet in a small, open area outside the classrooms, and students who see them together lose confidence in the counselor. They ask if he tells the teachers what they have told him.

Counselors must interact with teachers. That is not only because teachers are counselors' professional peers and provide daily adult contact, but because consulting with teachers is part of a counselor's job description. Students sometimes worry about conversations counselors have with teachers, especially if they have told the counselor something they do not want the teacher to know. This puts the counselor in a difficult position, because teacher contact is essential. So is students' trust.

Include a discussion of the meaning of *mutual trust* as part of an initial group session. You will trust the students, and you expect they will trust you unless you show them they cannot. Explain that having trust in oneself and in others is a part of everyday living and that, without trust, society could not exist. Give examples of what could happen if people did not have faith in others. If no one had faith in a pilot, no one would fly in an airplane. If no one had faith in a doctor, no one would go to a hospital. If no one had faith in other people, no one would have any friends.

When the group discusses *confidentiality*, counselors should mention how confidentiality affects their work. Students appreciate honesty. Tell the students that they may see you with teachers. Tell them what you talk about with the teachers. If coffee time is when you talk about your personal life, say so.

If you are consulting with a teacher about a member of the group, explain that doing so is part of your job. Emphasize that you will never reveal anything that students have told you in confidence unless you would be breaking the law by not reporting it to an authority.

Now ... Go forward! Use the included groups as presented or adapt them to meet your needs.

ASCA STANDARDS FOR GROUPS TO GO K-3	LISTENING	CONCENTRATION	REPEATERS	TIME MANAGEMENT	STUDY SKILLS	MAKING THE DECISION	ANGER	FACING REALITY	ATTENTION SEEKING	CONTROLLING ANGER	SELF-ESTEEM	SHYNESS	I'M SPECIAL	FRIENDSHIP
ACADEMIC DEVELOPMENT														
Standard A: Students will acquire the attitudes, knowledge, and skills that contribute to effective learning in school and across the life span.														
Competency A:1 Improve Academic Self-Concept														
A/A:1.1 Articulate feelings of competence and confidence as a learner		■				■						■	■	
A/A:1.2 Display a positive interest in learning		■			■	■						■		
A/A:1.3 Take pride in work and in achievement		■		■	■	■						■		
A/A:1.4 Accept mistakes as essential to the learning process			■				■		■	■				
A/A:1.5 Identify attitudes and behaviors which lead to successful learning		■	■	■	■	■	■		■	■	■			
Competency A:2 Acquire Skills For Improving Learning														
A/A:2.1 Apply time-and task-management skills		■		■	■									
A/A:2.2 Demonstrate how effort and persistence positively affect learning				■	■	■	■							
A/A:2.3 Use communication skills to know when and how to ask for help when needed	■	■	■	■			■		■	■				
A/A:2.4 Apply knowledge of learning styles to positively influence school performance		■				■	■							
Competency A:3 Achieve School Success														
A/A:3.1 Take responsibility for own actions	■				■		■		■	■	■			
A/A:3.2 Demonstrate the ability to work independently, as well as the ability to work cooperatively with other students		■			■	■	■	■		■	■	■		■
A/A:3.3 Develop a broad range of interests and abilities						■					■		■	
A/A:3.4 Demonstrate dependability, productivity, and initiative		■			■	■					■	■		
A/A:3.5 Share knowledge		■			■	■		■		■	■	■	■	
Standard B: Students will complete school with the academic preparation essential to choose from a wide range of substantial postsecondary options, including college.														
Competency B:1 Improve Learning														
A/B:1.1 Demonstrate the motivation to achieve individual potential	■				■			■			■	■		
A/B:1.3 Apply the study skills necessary for academic success at each level	■				■						■			
A/B:1.7 Become self-directed and independent learners	■	■			■						■			
Competency B:2 Plan To Achieve Goals														
A/B:2.4 Apply knowledge of aptitudes and interests to goal setting											■	■	■	
A/B:2.5 Use problem-solving and decision-making skills to assess progress toward educational goals										■	■	■		
A/B:2.6 Understand the relationship between classroom performance and success in school	■	■	■		■					■	■			

ASCA STANDARDS FOR GROUPS TO GO K-3

	LISTENING	CONCENTRATION	REPEATERS	TIME MANAGEMENT	STUDY SKILLS	MAKING THE DECISION	ANGER	FACING REALITY	ATTENTION SEEKING	CONTROLLING ANGER	SELF-ESTEEM	SHYNESS	I'M SPECIAL	FRIENDSHIP
PERSONAL/SOCIAL DEVELOPMENT														
Standard A: Students will acquire knowledge, attitudes, and interpersonal skills to help them understand and respect self and others														
Competency A:1 Acquire Self-Knowledge														
PS/A:1.1 Develop a positive attitude toward self as a unique and worthy person	●	●	●					●			●	●	●	
PS/A:1.2 Identify values, attitudes, and beliefs			●					●			●	●	●	●
PS/A:1.4 Understand change as a part of growth			●					●		●	●			
PS/A:1.5 Identify and express feelings			●		●		●	●		●	●	●	●	●
PS/A:1.6 Distinguish between appropriate and inappropriate behaviors	●		●		●		●		●	●	●			
PS/A:1.7 Recognize personal boundaries, rights, and privacy needs					●		●		●	●	●			
PS/A:1.8 Understand the need for self-control and how to practice it	●		●		●		●		●	●	●			
PS/A:1.9 Demonstrate cooperative behavior in groups	●					●	●	●	●	●	●	●		●
PS/A:1.10 Identify personal strengths and assets	●	●	●							●	●	●	●	●
PS/A:1.11 Identify and discuss changing personal and social roles								●	●	●	●			●
PS/A:1.12 Identify and recognize changing family roles									●	●	●			
Competency A:2 Acquire Interpersonal Skills														
PS/A:2.1 Recognize that everyone has rights and responsibilities			●	●	●	●	●		●	●	●	●		
PS/A:2.2 Respect alternative points of view	●	●				●	●	●		●	●	●		●
PS/A:2.3 Recognize, accept, respect, and appreciate individual differences	●	●	●				●	●		●	●	●		●
PS/A:2.6 Use effective communication skills	●	●			●	●	●	●	●	●	●	●		●
PS/A:2.7 Know that communication involves speaking, listening, and nonverbal behavior	●	●			●	●	●		●	●	●	●		
PS/A:2.8 Learn to make and keep friends						●				●	●	●		●
Standard B: Students will make decisions, set goals, and take necessary action to achieve goals.														
Competency B:1 Self-Knowledge Applications														
PS/B:1.1 Use a decision-making and problem-solving model								●		●		●		
PS/B:1.2 Understand consequences of decisions and choices		●						●	●	●		●		
PS/B:1.3 Identify alternative solutions to a problem									●	●		●		
PS/B:1.4 Develop effective coping skills for dealing with problems			●				●	●	●	●				
PS/B:1.6 Know how to apply conflict-resolution skills							●			●				
PS/B:1.10 Identify alternative ways of achieving goals								●		●				
PS/B:1.11 Use persistence and perseverance in acquiring knowledge and skills	●				●	●								
PS/B:1.12 Develop an action plan to set and achieve realistic goals					●	●			●					
Standard C:Students will understand safety and survival skills.														
Competency C:1 Acquire Personal Safety Skills														
PS/C:1.3 Learn the difference between appropriate and inappropriate physical contact										●				
PS/C:1.4 Demonstrate the ability to assert boundaries, rights, and personal privacy					●					●				
PS/C:1.9 Learn how to cope with peer pressure			●				●							
PS/C:1.10 Learn techniques for managing stress and conflict							●			●				
PS/C:1.11 Learn coping skills for managing life events							●	●		●				

ACADEMIC IMPROVEMENT

Listening: A Study Skill (Grades K-3)

Concentration: A Study Skill (Grades K-3)

Another Year In The Same Grade (Repeaters-Grades K-3)

Time Management (Grades 2-3)

All Aboard The Study Skills Work Habits Express (Grades 1-3)

Making The Decision To Learn (Grades 1-3)

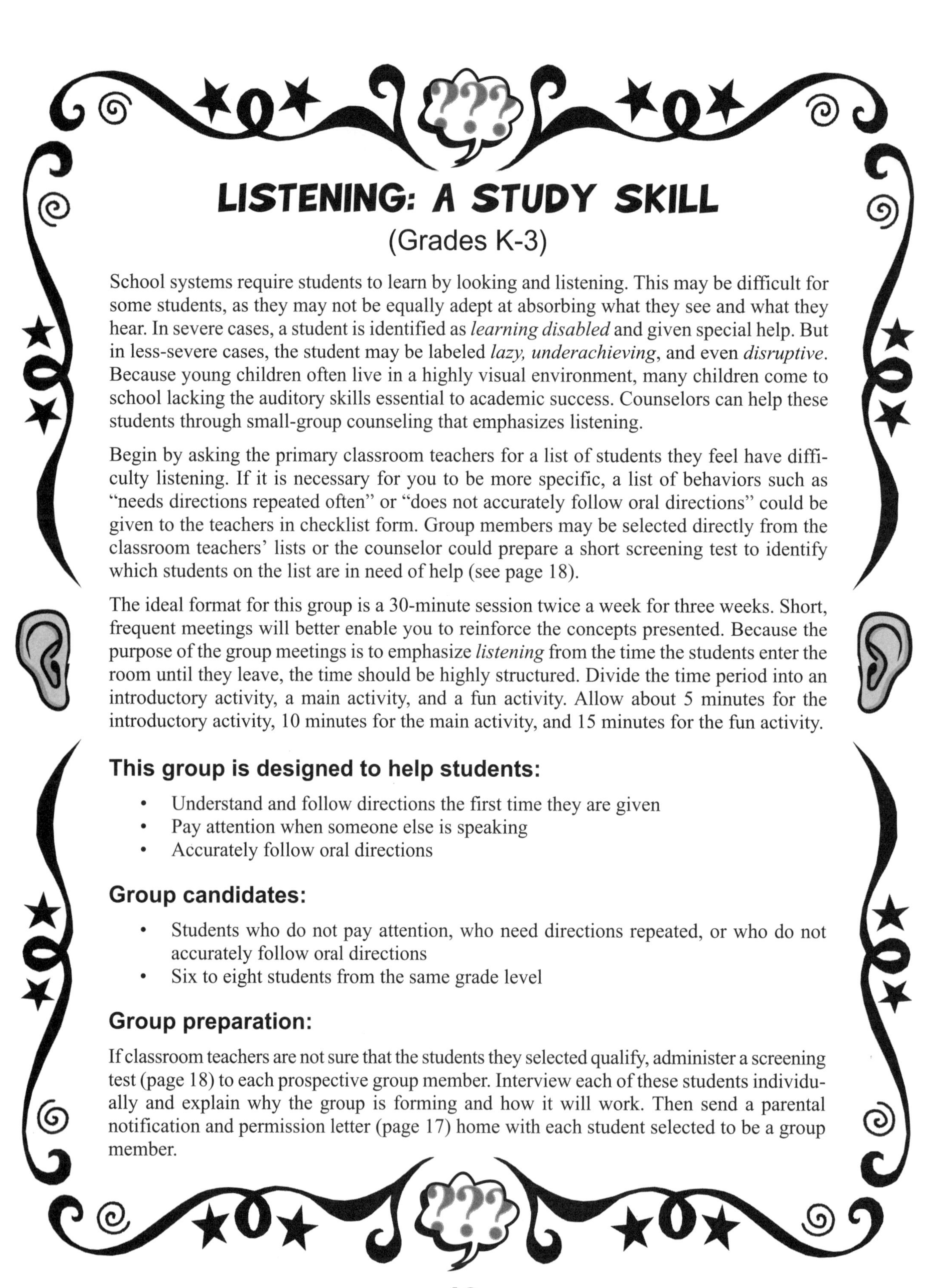

LISTENING: A STUDY SKILL

(Grades K-3)

School systems require students to learn by looking and listening. This may be difficult for some students, as they may not be equally adept at absorbing what they see and what they hear. In severe cases, a student is identified as *learning disabled* and given special help. But in less-severe cases, the student may be labeled *lazy, underachieving*, and even *disruptive*. Because young children often live in a highly visual environment, many children come to school lacking the auditory skills essential to academic success. Counselors can help these students through small-group counseling that emphasizes listening.

Begin by asking the primary classroom teachers for a list of students they feel have difficulty listening. If it is necessary for you to be more specific, a list of behaviors such as "needs directions repeated often" or "does not accurately follow oral directions" could be given to the teachers in checklist form. Group members may be selected directly from the classroom teachers' lists or the counselor could prepare a short screening test to identify which students on the list are in need of help (see page 18).

The ideal format for this group is a 30-minute session twice a week for three weeks. Short, frequent meetings will better enable you to reinforce the concepts presented. Because the purpose of the group meetings is to emphasize *listening* from the time the students enter the room until they leave, the time should be highly structured. Divide the time period into an introductory activity, a main activity, and a fun activity. Allow about 5 minutes for the introductory activity, 10 minutes for the main activity, and 15 minutes for the fun activity.

This group is designed to help students:

- Understand and follow directions the first time they are given
- Pay attention when someone else is speaking
- Accurately follow oral directions

Group candidates:

- Students who do not pay attention, who need directions repeated, or who do not accurately follow oral directions
- Six to eight students from the same grade level

Group preparation:

If classroom teachers are not sure that the students they selected qualify, administer a screening test (page 18) to each prospective group member. Interview each of these students individually and explain why the group is forming and how it will work. Then send a parental notification and permission letter (page 17) home with each student selected to be a group member.

Dear ____:

Listening skills are essential for academic success. Many factors contribute to the fact that a child has difficulty following directions, needs directions repeated often, and/or does not pay attention when someone is speaking. Children who cannot listen effectively do not get the most out of time spent in school.

Your child's classroom teacher has identified your child as a student who could benefit from extra help in learning to listen effectively.

In an effort to help your child and others learn to listen effectively, I am forming a counseling group that will focus on developing better listening skills. During our time together students will perform a variety of tasks to improve their listening skills.

The group will meet for 30 minutes twice a week for four weeks at a time arranged with the classroom teacher.

Your child knows about the group and has indicated that he or she would like to participate in it. However, no child is ever included in a small-group counseling program without his or her parents' knowledge and permission.

Please indicate, by completing the form below, that you wish to have your child participate in this group or that you do not want him or her to be included.

Return the permission slip to me by ___________________________.

Thank you,

✂- -

☐ I, ______________________________________, ***give permission*** for my child to participate in the small-group counseling program on listening skills.

☐ I, ______________________________________, ***do not give permission*** for my child to participate in the small-group counseling program on listening skills.

Child's Name ______________________________________ Date ________________

School ____ Grade ________________

Teacher ____

Home Phone (_____) ________________ Work Phone (_____) ________________

Parent's Printed Name ______________________________

Parent's Signature _________________________________

STUDENT SCREENING TEST

Name ______________________________________ Grade __________

Place a checkmark (✓) in the circle if the task was successfully completed.

Sequential Order:

Read the four words aloud. Then ask the student to repeat one of the words.

- ◯ kangaroo, tiger, lion, jellyfish — Name the second word I said.
- ◯ beets, beans, broccoli, bread — Name the third word I said.
- ◯ five, fifty, forty, four — Name the first word I said.
- ◯ cake and ice cream
  peanut butter and jelly
  hot dogs and mustard
  spaghetti and meat balls — Name the third set of words I said.

Figure Ground:

Turn on a CD or radio and play background music. Change the volume as you proceed down the list. Have the student do as you ask while the music is playing.

- ◯ Clap your hands five times.
- ◯ Walk to the door and back.
- ◯ Stand on one foot and count to 10.
- ◯ Close your eyes and wave your arms over your head.

Memorization:

Name four items. Have the students repeat the items in the order that they are named.

- ◯ shark, whale, dolphin, clam
- ◯ Sixteen, nineteen, twenty-five, sixty-six
- ◯ pretty, prim, practice, problem
- ◯ charge, change, cherry, chicken

INTRODUCTORY LISTENING ACTIVITIES

(*Note:* This small group's format is not presented the same way as the other groups in this book. Other groups present step-by-step directions for each session. Because each group session is divided into the same three parts, lists of activities appropriate for each part are listed together. From these lists, you may choose the activities best suited for the students in your group. By using this format, some activities may never be used. Others may be repeated if the leader deems it necessary. There are enough choices for six sessions.)

Objective:

To set an atmosphere conducive to listening

Materials Needed:

For each student:
- ☐ None

For the leader:
- ☑ Textbook used at the students' grade level (optional)
- ☑ Book of riddles (optional)

Activity Preparation:

Gather the necessary materials.

Introductory Activity: (5 Minutes)

- The introductory listening activity, presented immediately after the students enter the room, should be short and to the point. Choose one of the following activities:

1. Read a short paragraph from a textbook used at the students' grade level. Ask the students a question about a specific piece of information addressed in the paragraph.

2. Have the students make up a sentence in which each word begins with a certain letter. For example, "Susie swam swiftly so Sam said."

3. Have one student present a one-to two-minute autobiography. Then have the other students tell what they heard him/her say.

4. Tell the students to think of a color, an animal, etc. Have the first student say the word. Then the second student must say the first student's word and add his/her word. Each student repeats what the students before him/her said, adding words until the last person in the group has repeated what everyone said and has added a word.

5. Using a riddle book, tell the students a riddle. See if they can guess the answer.

6. Tell the students that instead of answering "here" when their name is called, they are to answer with their favorite food, a month of the year, etc. When each student has answered, ask one student to repeat what everyone has said.

MAIN LISTENING ACTIVITIES

Objective:

To concentrate on a particular listening skill such as *memorization, figure-ground,* or *sequential order*

Materials Needed:

For each student:

☑ Paper (optional)
☑ Pencil (optional)

For the leader:

☐ None

Activity Preparation:

Gather the necessary materials.

Main Activities: (10 Minutes)

- Select an activity from the *Memorization*, *Sequential Order*, or *Figure Ground* list. During the 10 minutes set aside for this part of the session, there should be no interruptions.

- *Memorization* activities:

  1. Have the students memorize lists of meaningful items, such as the names of their classmates, holidays during the year, months of the year, or days of the week.

  2. Have the students memorize group members' birthdates.

  3. Obtain the week's spelling words from the classroom teacher and have the students memorize the list.

  4. Play an addition/substraction game in which one student states the problem and the next student answers the problem, then starts the next problem with the answer just given. For example, if one student says 1 + 3, and the answering student says "4," that student must then start his/her problem with the number 4, such as 4 + 3 =. Limit the numbers that may be used. You might say, for example, that no problem may have an answer greater than 10.

- *Sequential Order* activities:

  1. Give each student a piece of paper and a pencil. Begin with a number comfortable for everyone in the group, such as three. Then say three words. Repeat one of the words and ask the students to write on the paper the number that tells when you said that word.

  2. Say a letter of the alphabet or a day of the week. Have the students tell what letter or day comes either before or after the one mentioned.

- *Figure Ground* activity:

  See if the students can block out background noises and continue to do what is expected of them. You can do this by playing a radio, a CD, or by turning on the television, then giving specific directions.

Listening: A Study Skill
FUN LISTENING ACTIVITIES

Objective:

To continue the *listening* lesson in a more subtle form

Materials Needed:

For each student:
- ☑ Art paper (optional)
- ☑ Crayons or markers (optional)

For the leader:
- ☑ Recording of a song which includes directions to be followed (optional)

Activity Preparation:

Gather the necessary materials.

Fun Activities: (15 Minutes)

- Suggested fun activities:
  1. Play *The Hokey Pokey* or other music that includes directions to be followed.
  2. Give the students art paper and crayons or markers. Give very specific drawing directions. The purpose of this activity is to see if all the students interpret the directions the same way or if they all draw different things.
  3. Have one student think of an animal, person, or place. The student should then describe whatever he/she chose to the group. The group should try to guess what or who the student is pretending to be.
  4. Play games like *Simon Says* or *Twenty Questions.*

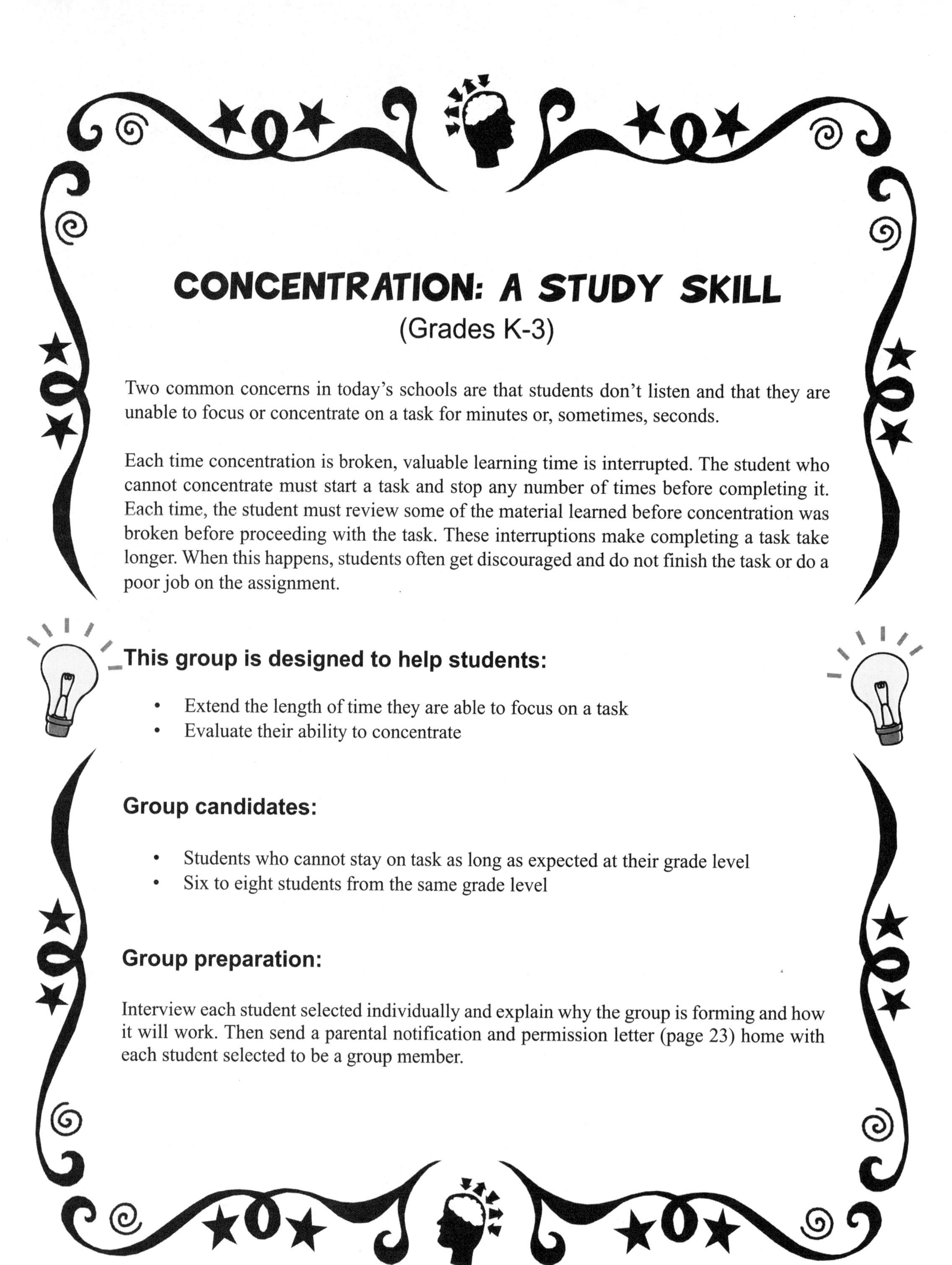

CONCENTRATION: A STUDY SKILL

(Grades K-3)

Two common concerns in today's schools are that students don't listen and that they are unable to focus or concentrate on a task for minutes or, sometimes, seconds.

Each time concentration is broken, valuable learning time is interrupted. The student who cannot concentrate must start a task and stop any number of times before completing it. Each time, the student must review some of the material learned before concentration was broken before proceeding with the task. These interruptions make completing a task take longer. When this happens, students often get discouraged and do not finish the task or do a poor job on the assignment.

This group is designed to help students:

- Extend the length of time they are able to focus on a task
- Evaluate their ability to concentrate

Group candidates:

- Students who cannot stay on task as long as expected at their grade level
- Six to eight students from the same grade level

Group preparation:

Interview each student selected individually and explain why the group is forming and how it will work. Then send a parental notification and permission letter (page 23) home with each student selected to be a group member.

Dear ____:

Academic success requires the ability to focus or concentrate on a task. It is difficult to pinpoint why one child can concentrate and another cannot, because many different factors can contribute to a child's difficulty in staying on task. Children who cannot concentrate effectively do not get the most out of the time they spend in school.

Your child's classroom teacher has identified your child as a student who could benefit from extra help in learning to concentrate on tasks.

In an effort to help your child and others overcome this difficulty, I am forming a counseling group that will focus on helping students improve their ability to concentrate. Students who participate in this group will explore a variety of tasks that will improve their ability to focus.

The group will meet for 30 minutes a week for four weeks at a time arranged with the classroom teacher.

Your child knows about the group and has indicated that he or she would like to participate in it. However, no child is ever included in a small-group counseling program without his or her parents' knowledge and permission.

Please indicate, by completing the form below, that you wish to have your child participate in this group or that you do not want him or her to be included.

Return the permission slip to me by ________________________.

Thank you,

✂- -

☐ I, ______________________________________, ***give permission*** for my child to participate in the small-group counseling program on concentration.

☐ I, ______________________________________, ***do not give permission*** for my child to participate in the small-group counseling program on concentration.

Child's Name ________________________________ Date ____________

School ________________________________ Grade ____________

Teacher ________________________________

Home Phone (____) ______________ Work Phone (____) ______________

Parent's Printed Name ________________________________

Parent's Signature ________________________________

INTRODUCTORY CONCENTRATION ACTIVITIES

(*Note:* This small group's format is not presented the same way as the other groups in this book. Other groups present step-by-step directions for each session. Because each group session begins in the same manner, the introductory session will be repeated throughout the entire group experience. Each group concludes in the same way, which is repeated through the entire group experience. The *Focusing Power Activities* are varied. Leaders may choose to use one or more for each group session.)

Objective:

To prepare the students to concentrate for a longer period of time

Materials Needed:

For each student:

- ☑ Copy of *Personal Concentration Chart* (page 25)
- ☑ Pencil

For the leader:

- ☑ Clock or watch

Activity Preparation:

Reproduce the *Personal Concentration Chart* for each student. Gather the other necessary materials.

Introductory Activity: (5 Minutes)

- Give each student a *Personal Concentration Chart* and a pencil. Tell the students that on this personal chart they will record the amount of time they will concentrate on the activities presented during these sessions.
- Have the students write their names on their charts, then review its contents.
- Select a topic or object, such as their shoes, for the students to focus on.
- Explain the focusing activity. Tell the students how much time they will spend on the activity (maximum of five minutes). Then have the students write down the title of the activity and the length of time they believe they will be able to concentrate on the activity.
- Tell the students to raise their hands the moment they have any distracting thoughts. When a student raises his/her hand, give him/her a number to write on his/her activity sheet in the *Time* column. The student should again begin to concentrate on the activity until the allotted time has elapsed.

PERSONAL CONCENTRATION CHART

Concentration: A Study Skill
FOCUSING POWER ACTIVITIES

Objective:

To concentrate on a particular assignment

Materials Needed:

For each student:
- ☑ *Personal Concentration Chart* from previous session
- ☑ Pencil

For the leader:
- ☑ Clock or watch
- ☑ Varies, depending upon the activity chosen

Activity Preparation:

Gather any necessary materials associated with each activity.

Focusing Power Activities:

(20 Minutes)

- Begin the activity by having the students write the title of the next activity in the activity column on their *Personal Concentration* charts. Tell the students that if they break concentration at any time during an activity, they should raise their hands. You will then tell them what number to place in their time column. This does not mean the activity will stop. It only means they will record the length of time they were able to focus without breaking concentration. Select one of the following activities.

COLOR COMMUNICATION

Materials Needed: None

- Have each student select a color he/she feels is important.
- Divide the students into pairs. Have each student spend three minutes telling his/her partner the various reasons why the color he/she selected is important. Call "time" after three minutes. Then have the partner who was the listener become the speaker and the partner who was the speaker become the listener.
- Conclude the activity by having the students share their best idea about the color and their partner's best idea.

SOUNDS

Materials Needed: Drawing paper and crayons for each student

- Have the students lie on the floor, close their eyes (optional), and count and identify all the sounds they hear. (*Note:* Select an amount of time for this part of the activity that is appropriate for the group members' age. You may choose a certain number of sounds for the students to identify.)
- When the allotted time has elapsed, distribute drawing paper and crayons to the students. Have the students draw pictures of their environment, using only illustrations related to sounds they heard. (This results in interesting pictures, as the usual things included—such as grass, trees, and sky—cannot be used unless they were heard.)

- Have the students exchange the pictures. Then have the student to whom each picture was given tell a story about it.

LISTENING TO MY MIND

Materials Needed: None

- Have the students lie on the floor and close their eyes (optional), and concentrate for five minutes. Tell the students they may hear sounds or words or see pictures in their minds. Tell them to be prepared to describe what they have heard or seen.

- When the allotted time has elapsed, have the students describe what they saw or heard in their minds. After each thing is mentioned, have the student attach a feeling word or phrase that describes his/her personal thoughts.

REMEMBERING

Materials Needed: Drawing paper and crayons for each student

- Have each student remember something that happened before he/she came to school. Each student should give a detailed description of the event.

- Distribute drawing paper and crayons to each student. Select one of the events named. Have each student draw a picture of the event, then describe his/her picture to the rest of the group. (These descriptions will give the group good examples of different ways that different people can interpret the same incident.)

POETRY:

Materials Needed: 2 poems of equal length

- Ask two group members to read aloud two different poems at the same time to the group. The poems should be approximately the same length.

- Have the other group members choose one of the readers and listen only to that student, ignoring the other reader.

- Then have the group brainstorm all the different times that they heard more than one sound. Discuss the things that cause someone to be distracted and how they feel about being distracted.

Concentration: A Study Skill
CONCLUSION

Objective:

To have the students evaluate their ability to concentrate

Materials Needed:

For each student:
☐ None

For the leader:
☐ None

Concluding Activity: (5 Minutes)

- Have the students tell the group what they recorded on their *Personal Concentration Charts*. Have each student evaluate the difference between what he/she felt he/she could accomplish and what he/she actually did accomplish.

- Tell the students they may take their *Personal Concentration Charts* home.

ANOTHER YEAR IN THE SAME GRADE

(Way To Help Repeaters—Grades K-3)

In most schools each year, some students are retained at the same grade level. This could be due to immaturity, chronological age, undue absenteeism, illness, moving from a district which progressed more slowly, inability or lack of interest in completing work at a grade level due to such psychological problems as parents' divorcing or child abuse, etc. Whatever the reasons for the retention, the students who are retained often have feelings of failure, disappointment, frustration, and anxiety about their future.

There are several things the counselor can do to help make the retention a more positive experience:

1. Work with parents to help them deal positively with their child
2. Work in the classroom to help students better understand retention and other school problems
3. Work in small groups to help students who are repeating a grade level better understand and deal with their retention

This group is designed to help students:

- See retention as a positive experience
- Realize they are not alone
- Openly share their feelings
- Improve socialization skills and self-confidence

Group candidates:

- Students who are being retained
- Select the appropriate number of students being retained at one grade level (*Note:* If there are not enough students being retained at one grade level, combine Grades 1, 2, and 3.)

Group preparation:

Interview each student selected individually and explain why the group is forming and how it will work. Then send a parental notification and permission letter (page 30) home with each student selected to be a group member.

Dear ____,

Being retained at the same grade level is a traumatic event for a young child. Children often do not understand why they are being retained and no matter how often they are told that why they are being retained is because they are young for the grade, missed too many days of school because of illness, or any other reason they still feel confused, embarrassed, and angry.

Students being retained need to know they are not alone. Their self-confidence often needs a boost. Your child's classroom teacher has identified your child as one of these students.

In an effort to help your child and others overcome this difficulty, I am forming a counseling group that will allow students who have been retained to explore their feelings, focus on their strengths, and learn how to deal with students who might be hurtful toward them.

The five group meetings will be held at a time the classroom teacher selects.

Your child knows about the group and has indicated that he or she would like to participate in it. However, no child is ever included in a small-group counseling program without his or her parents' knowledge and permission.

Please indicate, by completing the form below, that you wish to have your child participate in this group or that you do not want him or her to be included.

Return the permission slip to me by ________________________.

Thank you,

✂- -

☐ I, ____________________________________, ***give permission*** for my child to participate in the small-group counseling program to reduce retention anxiety.

☐ I, ____________________________________, ***do not give permission*** for my child to participate in the small-group counseling program to reduce retention anxiety.

Child's Name __________________________________ Date ______________

School ______________________________________ Grade ______________

Teacher ____________________________________

Home Phone (_____) _______________ Work Phone (_____) _______________

Parent's Printed Name ___________________________

Parent's Signature ______________________________

Session 1: Retention
WHY? AND HOW IT FEELS

Objective:

To elicit students' beliefs about why they were retained and how they feel about being retained

Materials Needed:

For each student:
- ☐ None

For the leader:
- ☐ None

Session Preparation:

None

Session:

- Introduce yourself and tell the students what day, time, and how many times the group will meet.
- Review the *Ground Rules* for group behavior.

  1. All group members will have an opportunity to share and to be heard.
  2. No negative comments or put-downs will be allowed.

- Have the students learn each others' names by paying the *Name Train Game*. Have one student begin by giving his/her name and the name of his/her favorite food. The next student repeats what the first student said, then states his/her name and favorite food. The process is repeated with every student in the group.
- Have the students share what grade they are in and what grade they were in the previous year. Discuss what repeating a grade level means.
- Read the following story aloud to the students:

  Kim had been looking forward to her friend Jennifer's sleepover for the past week. It was Jennifer's birthday, and she had asked Kim and five other girls who did everything together to come over. The day before the sleepover, Kim's mother was called to school for a conference with Kim's teacher and the school counselor. Kim couldn't imagine why her mom was going to school, because she knew she had not done anything wrong. When her mother came home, Kim immediately wanted to know what was going on. At first, her mother said it was nothing too important. But Kim begged and begged until her mother finally told her something she had never expected to hear. Mother began by telling Kim that her teacher really liked her and thought she had a lot of ability. But because Kim was younger than most of the students in her grade, she just couldn't keep up with the work. That made no sense to Kim, because she knew she got most of her work done. It took her longer, but that was only because she wanted to be sure it was right. At least that is what Kim thought. "What else did Mrs. Cramer say?" asked Kim. Kim's mother told her that her teacher and the counselor felt the best thing would be for Kim to repeat the grade. Kim could not believe what she was hearing!

- Ask the students:

  Why were you retained?

  Listen carefully to each student's response. Be sure to refute any incorrect reasons.

- Ask the students how they feel about being retained and how the other students in the class treat them. (*Note:* If any students mention being teased, say that in the next session, the group will talk about what to do about teasing.)

- Have the students share any feelings or concerns they have about repeating a grade.

- Conclude the session by having each student complete the following statement:

  Two things I am good at are _____ .

Session 2: Retention
FACING FRIENDS

Objective:

To discuss how students who have been retained are treated by other students

Materials Needed:

For each student:
☐ None

For the leader:
☑ Chalkboard and chalk or chart paper and marker

Session Preparation:

Gather the necessary materials.

Session:

- Begin again with the *Name Train Game*, adding the students' favorite colors to their names and favorite foods.

- Continue reading aloud the story from Session 1:

  Kim had been looking forward to her friend Jennifer's sleepover for the past week. It was Jennifer's birthday, and she had asked Kim and five other girls who did everything together to come over. Now everything had changed. Kim would not be in the same classroom as the other girls. They would not talk about assignments given out. They would not be in music, art, or gym together. In the cafeteria, they would not eat together. Kim would be at a different table. It was awful. And now she had to face everyone at Jennifer's birthday sleepover. She wondered if they knew. She wondered if she should tell them. She wondered what they would say if she did tell them. Would they still want her to be part of their group? Or would she be an outsider? Would they turn on her and tease her because she had to spend another year in the same grade? It just wasn't fair!

- Ask the students:

  How do you think Kim feels? (Kim feels angry, embarrassed, confused, hurt, and any other appropriate answers.)

  Do any of you have these feelings?

  How did your friends treat you?

- If any of the students mention being treated poorly, have those who wish to do so share any incidents of poor treatment or teasing by other students. As the students are sharing, their experiences, encourage them to talk about their feelings.

- Discuss both negative and positive ways students handle being teased in any situation. Make a special point of discussing being teased about being retained. Write the students' suggestions on the board or chart paper. Some reactions that might be mentioned include:

  Hit the teaser.
  Call the teaser other names.
  Ignore the teasing.
  Tell an adult.
  Explain why you were retained.
  Tell another student who can help you.
  Throw something at the teaser.
  Cry or pout.

- Have members of the group take turns role-playing each of the reactions to teasing that the group has named. After each role-play, discuss how the teaser and the person being teased felt in each situation.
- Have the group members describe what they feel are the best ways to handle teasing.
- Conclude the session by suggesting that the students practice using responses to teasing that will not get them into trouble.

Session 3: Retention
FEELINGS

Objective:

To identify things that make the students feel bad and things that make them feel good

Materials Needed:

For each student:

☑ Large sheet of drawing paper
☑ Crayons or markers

For the leader:

☐ None

Session Preparation:

Gather the necessary materials.

Session:

- Begin the session by having the students describe any teasing situations they experienced since the previous session and have them describe what they did when the situation occurred. Reinforce the positive responses to teasing identified in the previous session.
- Ask the students how they feel when they are being teased.
- Have the students name other things that make them feel bad.
- Discuss things that make the students feel good.
- Distribute a large sheet of drawing paper and crayons or markers to each student. Have the students fold the paper in half. At the top of the paper the students should write *Things That Make Me Feel....* Below the title, they should write *Good* on one half of the paper and *Bad* on the other half.
- Tell the students to draw as many pictures as they can on each half of the paper, illustrating things that make them feel good or bad.
- After the pictures are drawn, explain that everyone has a right to feel good and bad about things. Explain that people should be able to talk about their good and bad feelings.
- Have the students share their drawings with the group.
- Collect the drawings and any distributed materials. Conclude the session by discussing things the students can do to make themselves feel good.

Session 4: Retention
STRENGTHS

Objective:

To have the students identify their strengths

Materials Needed:

For each student:

☑ Copy of *My Strengths* (page 37 or 38)
☑ Crayons or markers

Session Preparation:

Select which copy of *My Strengths* to use with the group, then reproduce the activity sheet for each student. Gather any other necessary materials.

Session:

- Discuss any good things that have happened to the students since the previous session.
- Ask if anyone is still being teased by other students.
- Discuss how remembering good things can help students forget about teasing and other bad things.
- Distribute *My Strengths* and crayons or markers to each student. Tell the students:
    1. In Section 1, draw or write something you do well in school.
    2. In Section 2, draw or write something you do well at home.
    3. In Section 3, draw or write something you do well with your friends.
    4. In Section 4, draw or write something else you do well.
- Have the students share their drawings or what they have written with the group.
- Collect the drawings and any other materials that were distributed.
- Discuss how someone feels when he/she does something well and how someone can help others realize when they are doing something well.
- Conclude the session by suggesting that each student should compliment someone who has done something well at least once each day before the next session.

Name ______________________________ Date ____________________

Name_______________________________ Date_________________

Session 5: Retention
CULMINATION AND EVALUATION

Objective:

To allow the students to give feedback about the group experience

Materials Needed:

For each student:

☑ Drawing paper
☑ Crayons or markers

For the leader:

☑ Students' drawings from previous sessions

Session Preparation:

Gather the necessary materials.

Session:

- Have the students describe what happened when they complimented another person and describe any other pertinent experiences they have had since the previous session.

- Distribute drawing paper and crayons or markers to each student. Tell the students to draw a picture of someone or something they would like to be.

- Have each student show his/her completed picture to the group, then have the other students guess what or who the picture represents. Each student should explain why he/she would like to be the person or thing drawn.

- After each student has presented his/her picture, have the other students describe one thing they like about the student showing the picture.

- To assess the value of the group and give the students a chance to verbalize any concerns they still have about having been retained and how they feel about themselves, ask:

    1. What did you like best about our meetings?

    2. Did you like attending group sessions?

    3. How did you feel when you first heard you were going to repeat a grade?

    4. How do you feel about it now?

    5. What would you say to a student who found out he or she was going to repeat a grade?

- Conclude the session by making a positive statement about each member of the group. Let the group members know when you are available if they wish to talk about any problems. Return the students' drawings for them to take home.

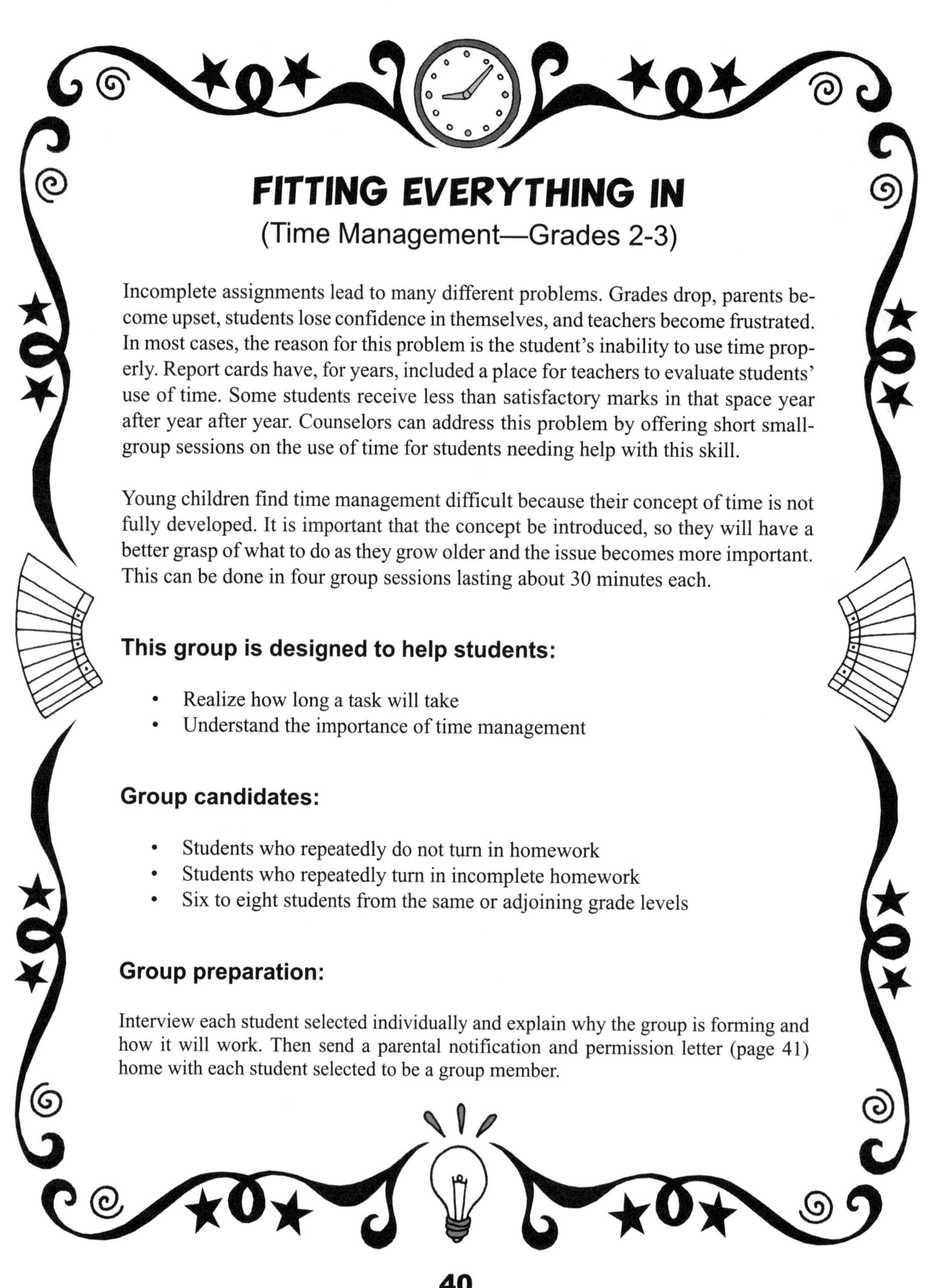

FITTING EVERYTHING IN

(Time Management—Grades 2-3)

Incomplete assignments lead to many different problems. Grades drop, parents become upset, students lose confidence in themselves, and teachers become frustrated. In most cases, the reason for this problem is the student's inability to use time properly. Report cards have, for years, included a place for teachers to evaluate students' use of time. Some students receive less than satisfactory marks in that space year after year after year. Counselors can address this problem by offering short small-group sessions on the use of time for students needing help with this skill.

Young children find time management difficult because their concept of time is not fully developed. It is important that the concept be introduced, so they will have a better grasp of what to do as they grow older and the issue becomes more important. This can be done in four group sessions lasting about 30 minutes each.

This group is designed to help students:

- Realize how long a task will take
- Understand the importance of time management

Group candidates:

- Students who repeatedly do not turn in homework
- Students who repeatedly turn in incomplete homework
- Six to eight students from the same or adjoining grade levels

Group preparation:

Interview each student selected individually and explain why the group is forming and how it will work. Then send a parental notification and permission letter (page 41) home with each student selected to be a group member.

Dear ____:

Time management is a difficult concept for many young children to grasp. They believe they can complete an assignment in less time than it will really take and, when they realize they can't, do a sloppy job, hand in incomplete work, or hand in no homework at all.

To receive the education they deserve, students need to know how to manage their time. If they do not learn to manage their time well, they will not reach their academic potential. Your child has been identified by his or her classroom teacher as a student who does not manage time effectively.

In an effort to help your child and others overcome this difficulty, I am forming a counseling group that will help students learn to manage homework time. Students in this group will practice estimating how long an assignment will take, doing the assignment, and comparing the time they thought the assignment would take to the amount of time it actually took.

There will be four group meetings, held at a time the classroom teacher selects.

Your child knows about the group and has indicated that he or she would like to participate in it. However, no child is ever included in a small-group counseling program without his or her parents' knowledge and permission.

Please indicate, by completing the form below, that you wish to have your child participate in this group or that you do not want him or her to be included.

Return the permission slip to me by ________________________.

Thank you,

✂- -

☐ I, ______________________________________, ***give permission*** for my child to participate in the small-group counseling program on time management.

☐ I, ______________________________________, ***do not give permission*** for my child to participate in the small-group counseling program on time management.

Child's Name ___________________________________ Date ______________

School ____ Grade _____________

Teacher _______________________________________

Home Phone (_____) _______________ Work Phone (_____) _______________

Parent's Printed Name ___________________________

Parent's Signature ______________________________

Session 1: Time Management
ESTIMATING TIME FOR A TASK

Objective:

To teach the students to realize the difference between the time they think it will take to do a task and the actual time it takes to do the task

Materials Needed:

For each student:

- ☑ Copy of *Clock Hands* (page 43)
- ☑ Paper plate
- ☑ Marker
- ☑ Brass fastener

For the leader:

- ☑ Copy of *Clock Hands* (page 43)
- ☑ Tagboard or cardstock
- ☑ Scissors
- ☑ Paper plate
- ☑ Marker
- ☑ Brass fastener
- ☑ Pencil
- ☑ Piece of paper

Session Preparation:

Reproduce *Clock Hands* on tagboard or cardstock for each student and the leader. Cut out the clock hands. Make a sample clock to show the students. Gather any other necessary materials.

Session:

- Ask the students to introduce themselves, then describe one way that clocks help them.
- Give each student a paper plate, marker, clock hands, and a brass fastener.
- Ask the students to tell how long they think it will take them to make their clocks. On a piece of paper, record the name of each student and the time he/she mentions.
- Show the students the sample clock and give them instructions on how to make the clocks. Allow them to begin. Tell them to put their names on their clocks and raise their hands when they are finished.
- As the students raise their hands, record the time each student took to make his/her clock.
- Conclude the lesson by discussing the difference in the amount of time each student thought it would take to make the clock and the amount of time it actually took. Discuss why these time differences occurred.
- Collect the clocks and save them for the next session. Collect any other materials that were distributed.

CLOCK HANDS

Punch a hole
and insert brad.

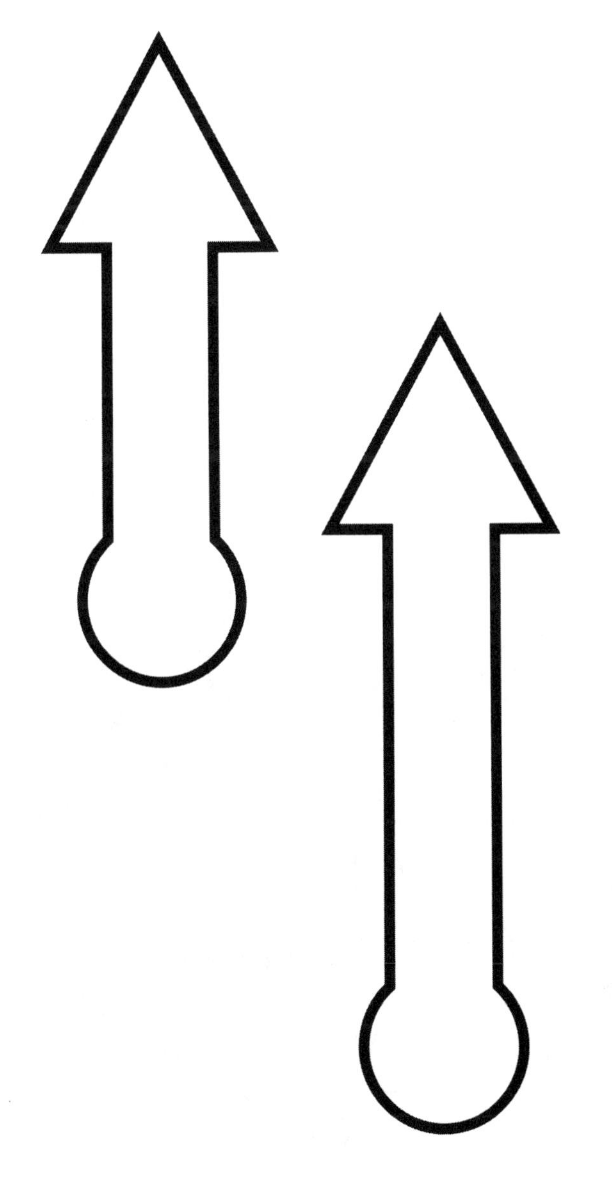

CLOCK HANDS

Punch a hole
and insert brad.

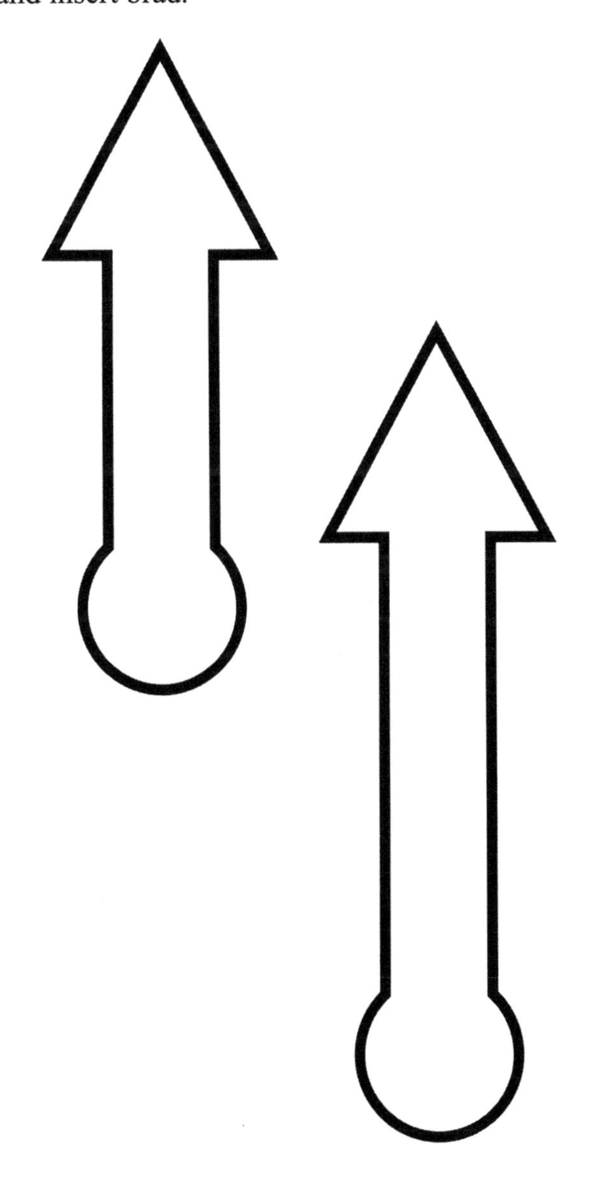

Session 2: Time Management
HOMEWORK AND TIME MANAGEMENT

Objective:

To teach the students to realize the importance of setting time aside to do homework

Materials Needed:

For each student:

☑ Clocks made in Session 1

For the leader:

☑ Selection of as many different kinds of clocks as possible (e.g., watch, alarm clock, stopwatch, teaching clock used in classrooms, digital clock, etc.)

Session Preparation:

Gather the necessary materials. Place the clocks where they can easily be seen by the students.

Session:

- Show and discuss the uses of all the different types of clocks.
- Ask the students why they think each clock is important. (By now, the students should understand that clocks help them accomplish things. Clocks help them know when to get up, when to eat dinner, when to go to school, when to watch their favorite TV show, etc.)
- Distribute the clocks the students made in the previous session.
- Have the students position the hands at various times of the day when they do things. (When they get up in the morning, leave for school, eat lunch, arrive home from school, watch TV, play with friends, eat dinner, go to bed, etc.)
- Ask the students to set the hands on the clock at the time they do their homework. (*Note:* Some will be able to do this. Others will have difficulty.)
- Have the students discuss why homework is important. Lead the discussion about why time should be set aside to do homework. Have the students look at their clocks and explain why the time on their clocks is a good time for them to do their homework.
- Conclude the session by telling the students to bring a library book to the next session.
- Collect the clocks.

Session 3: Time Management

ASSIGNMENTS AND TIME MANAGEMENT

Objective:

To teach the students to practice estimating how much time is needed to complete an assignment

Materials Needed:

For each student:

- ☑ Clocks from Session 1
- ☑ Pencil
- ☑ Paper
- ☑ Library book

For the leader:

- ☑ Chalkboard and chalk or chart paper and marker
- ☑ Textbooks from the students' grade level
- ☑ Piece of paper
- ☑ Pencil

Session Preparation:

Write on the board/chart paper a homework assignment that would take about 30 minutes to complete. Use the grade-level textbooks as a guide, and include more than one subject. The first assignment should be for the students to read their library books. Then add assignments such as math problems, writing four sentences, spelling words to study, etc. Gather any other necessary materials.

Session:

- Tell the students that during this session, they will practice managing their homework time.
- Distribute the students' clocks.
- Tell the students to select a 30-minute time period after arriving home in which to do their homework (If that time is inappropriate for anyone in the group, have those students select a more appropriate time.) Have the students set the hands on their clocks to the chosen time.
- Distribute paper and pencil to the students. Tell the students to take out their library books. Then tell them to look at the entire homework assignment on the board/chart paper. The first part of the assignment is to read from their library books.
- Explain that they will have 30 minutes to complete the entire assignment. Have each student select a certain amount of time from the 30-minute time period to work on each portion of the homework assignment.
- Have each student tell how much time he/she selected to read his/her library book and approximately how many pages he/she believes he/she will read during that time. Record the students' answers on a piece of paper.
- Tell the students that some of them will finish reading their selected number of pages before their time is up and that others will not. Explain that they should raise their hands if they read the selected number of pages before time is called. You will record how long it took each student to read the selected number of pages and the student should continue working on with the assignment. Tell those who do not finish before their time is up that you will call "Time" when the clock reaches the amount of time they selected. At that time, they should tell how many pages

they have read. You will record that number and they should continue working on the assignment.

- Have the students open their library books and begin reading.

- Allow the students to continue working on the assignment until 30 minutes have elapsed.

- Discuss how the amount of time each student set aside compared with the amount of time they actually needed to complete the assignment. Discuss what needs to be done by those students who did not complete as much as they thought they would and what needs to be done by those students who completed more than they thought they would.

- Conclude the session by asking the students to do this exercise each night at home. They should decide how much time they need for each homework subject, make a note of the time they think they will need, then write down how much time they needed to complete each homework subject. Tell them to bring these papers to the next session.

- Allow the students to take their clocks home with them. Collect any materials that were distributed.

Session 4: Time Management
EVALUATING TIME MANAGEMENT

Objective:

To help students understand the value of time management

Materials Needed:

For each student:
☑ Homework assignment from Session 3

For the leader:
☐ None

Session Preparation:

None

Session:

- Have each student share with the group the homework assignment from Session 3.
- Discuss as a group how accurately the students determined the amount of time needed for each assignment and whether they became more accurate as they practiced the task.
- Ask the group all or some of the following questions:

  What things do you like to spend time doing?

  Why does schoolwork take time?

  If you were not doing schoolwork, what might you be doing?

  How can time be wasted during school?

  Do you believe it is hard not to play during school time?

  What would you have to do if you wanted to play during time set aside for schoolwork?

  Tell us how you think you would feel if you could say everyday, "I did all my work on time."

- Conclude the group by telling the students that in order to complete their assignments on time, they should continue to do this exercise each night. They should decide how much time each assignment will take, work for that amount of time, then decide whether they gave themselves too much, too little, or just the right amount of time to complete the work. If they continue to do this, they will soon know how much time they must spend in order to finish their assignments and be able to plan accordingly.

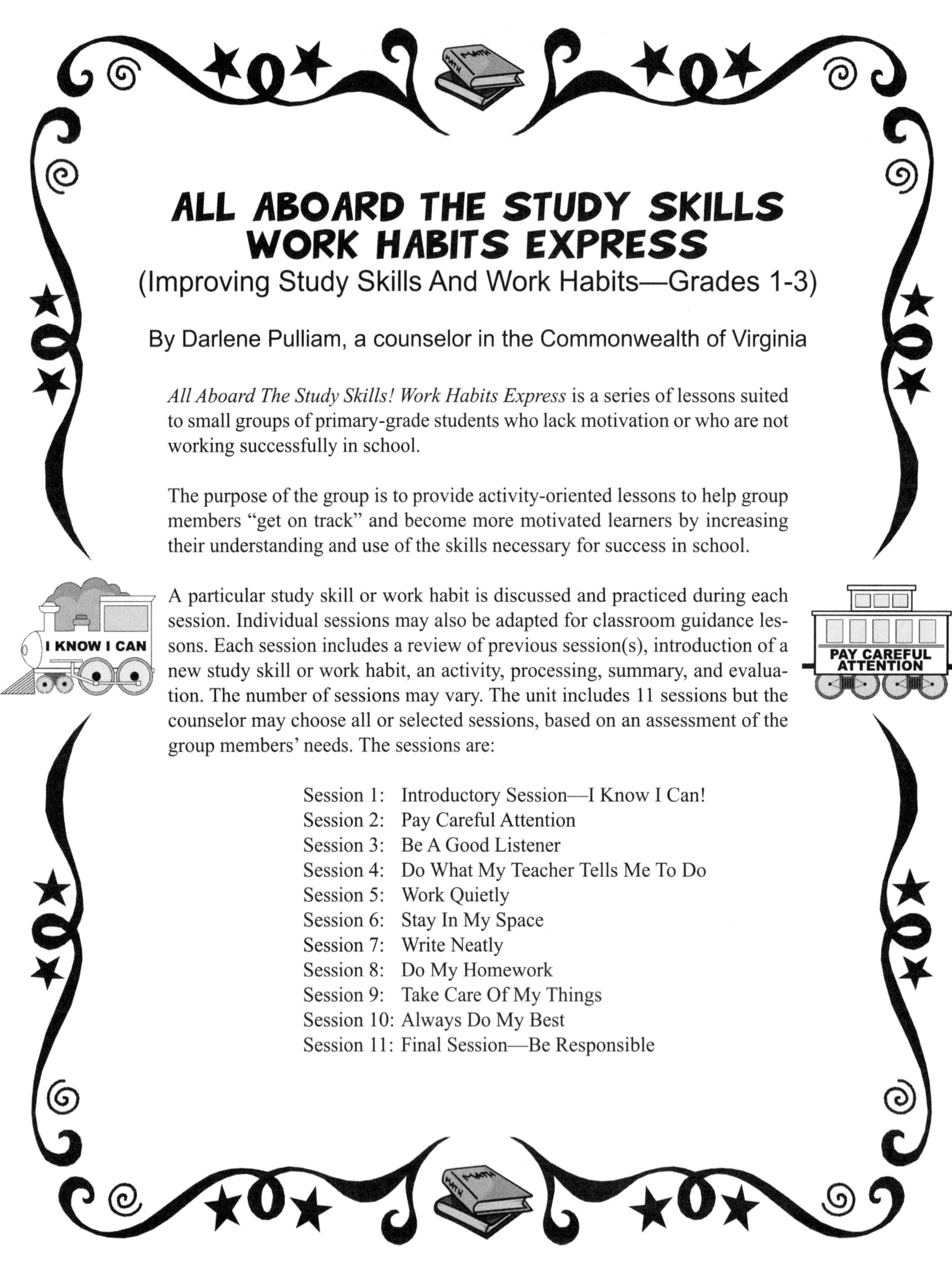

ALL ABOARD THE STUDY SKILLS WORK HABITS EXPRESS

(Improving Study Skills And Work Habits—Grades 1-3)

By Darlene Pulliam, a counselor in the Commonwealth of Virginia

All Aboard The Study Skills! Work Habits Express is a series of lessons suited to small groups of primary-grade students who lack motivation or who are not working successfully in school.

The purpose of the group is to provide activity-oriented lessons to help group members "get on track" and become more motivated learners by increasing their understanding and use of the skills necessary for success in school.

A particular study skill or work habit is discussed and practiced during each session. Individual sessions may also be adapted for classroom guidance lessons. Each session includes a review of previous session(s), introduction of a new study skill or work habit, an activity, processing, summary, and evaluation. The number of sessions may vary. The unit includes 11 sessions but the counselor may choose all or selected sessions, based on an assessment of the group members' needs. The sessions are:

Session 1: Introductory Session—I Know I Can!
Session 2: Pay Careful Attention
Session 3: Be A Good Listener
Session 4: Do What My Teacher Tells Me To Do
Session 5: Work Quietly
Session 6: Stay In My Space
Session 7: Write Neatly
Session 8: Do My Homework
Session 9: Take Care Of My Things
Session 10: Always Do My Best
Session 11: Final Session—Be Responsible

This group is designed to help students:

- Improve their work habits, resulting in more successful learning and better grades
- Motivate themselves to want to improve their work habits and study skills

Group candidates:

- Students who lack motivation
- Students who are not working successfully in school
- Five to eight students from the same or adjoining grade levels

Group preparation:

- Interview each student selected individually and explain why the group is forming and how it will work. Then send a parental notification and permission letter (page 50) home with each student selected to be a group member.

- **Folders:** Make a construction paper folder for each student. Staple a copy of *Toot Your Own Horn, Be A Successful Group Member* (page 51) to the inside of each folder.

- **Train Car Worksheets:** Color, laminate, and tape together a train that includes worksheets from the planned sessions (pages 54, 58, 61, 66, 69, 73, 76, 79, 82, 85, and 89). This laminated train may be used for demonstration and a group member may read from it aloud during the review and the summary times. Attach the completed train to a space where the students can see it and where it can remain for the duration of the group.

- **Evaluation Procedure:** At the end of each session, each group member will be evaluated. A student who has taken part in group activities, cooperated with other group members, listened, taken turns, and been helpful to the group, will receive a smiley face in one of the train windows on the *Toot Your Own Horn—Be A Successful Group Member* worksheet. The leader may draw the smiley face or use a sticker.

Dear ____:

School is not always a pleasant place for children who lack motivation or who are not achieving success. When this happens at an early age and is ignored, going to school can be drudgery. School can become a place the student *must* spend time during the day. To receive the education they deserve, students must know how to study effectively. Those who do not will not reach their academic potential.

Every young child deserves the best a school has to offer. That is why it is important for every child to have the study skills necessary for success. Your child's classroom teacher has identified your child as a student who can benefit from learning to study effectively.

To help your child and others, I am forming a counseling group that will focus on these important skills. Our group will be emphasizing paying attention, listening, working quietly, writing neatly, doing homework, and being responsible.

The 11 group meetings will last approximately 30-minutes each, and will be held at a time the classroom teacher selects.

Your child knows about the group and has indicated that he or she would like to participate in it. However, no child is ever included in a small-group counseling program without his or her parents' knowledge and permission.

Please indicate, by completing the form below, that you wish to have your child participate in this group or that you do not want him or her to be included.

Return the permission slip to me by ___________________________.

Thank you,

✂- -

☐ I, ____, ***give permission*** for my child to participate in the small-group counseling program for improving work habits and study skills.

☐ I, ____, ***do not give permission*** for my child to participate in the small-group counseling program for improving work habits and study skills.

Child's Name ______________________________________ Date _______________

School ____ Grade _______________

Teacher ____

Home Phone (_____) _______________ Work Phone (_____) _______________

Parent's Printed Name ______________________________

Parent's Signature _________________________________

TOOT YOUR OWN HORN

Session 1: Work Habits
INTRODUCTORY LESSON—I KNOW I CAN!

Objective:

To motivate students through positive self-talk and to encourage them to think about "getting on track" with better study skills and work habits

Materials Needed:

For each student:

- ☑ Folder
- ☑ Copy of *I Know I Can* (page 54)
- ☑ Pencil
- ☑ Crayons or markers

For the leader:

- ☑ *The Little Engine That Could* book
- ☑ Tagboard or cardstock
- ☑ Copy of *Motivational Reminder* (page 55)
- ☑ Laminator and laminating material
- ☑ Tape
- ☑ Smiley face stamp, smiley face stickers, or pencil
- ☑ Chart paper and marker

Session Preparation:

Obtain a copy of *The Little Engine That Could* from the library. (*Note:* If the book is unavailable, tell the story to the children.) Reproduce a *Motivational Reminder* for each student on tagboard/cardstock and laminate it for durability. Reproduce *I Know I Can* for each student. Gather any other necessary materials.

Session:

- Introduce the group by telling the students they will be meeting with you to learn how to work better in class.
- Explain any group rules you would like the students to follow, emphasizing confidentiality. Group members may share anything they have said with family or friends, but they are not allowed to reveal anything another group member has said to someone who is not in the group.

- Read or tell the story *The Little Engine That Could.* Discuss the story by asking:

  How did the little engine succeed?

  What kept the other engines from succeeding?

  How did saying "I think I can" help the little engine?

  What would have happened if the little engine did not try to pull the train?

  How would the children on the other side of the mountain have felt?

  What helpful words or thoughts, other than "I think I can," can we say to ourselves to help us not give up or to help us try new things? (Write these words or phrases on the chart paper.)

- Have the group members share stories about how they succeeded because they did not give up.

- Distribute a folder, *I Know I Can*, a pencil, and crayons or markers to each student. Have the students look at the *Toot Your Own Horn, Be A Successful Group Member* train engine worksheet stapled to the inside of their folders. Explain that at the end of each session, every group member who follows the group rules and contributes to the group process will earn a smiley face in one window of the train.

- Ask the group members to look at the laminated train engine on the wall. Have them read aloud the words *I Know I Can.*

- Ask the students to write some of the positive words or phrases from the chart paper on their *I Know I Can* worksheets. Then have them decorate their train engines.

- Have the students put their names on their folders and place the *I Know I Can* worksheet in their folders.

- Distribute a *Motivational Reminder* and tape to each student.

- Tell the students that the purpose of the notecards is for them to always have a reminder to try hard and not give up. When they return to their classrooms, they should tape the notecards to their desks and look at the notecards as they do their schoolwork.

- Continue the lesson by asking:

  Think about a time you gave up because you couldn't do something you tried to do. How did you feel?

  How did others react to your decision to give up?

  Think about a time when you finally succeeded in doing something you didn't think you could. How did you feel?

  How did others react to your decision to keep trying until you succeeded?

  What helped you succeed?

- Conclude the session by emphasizing the importance of thinking positively. Give the students who fulfilled the necessary requirements a smiley face on their *Toot Your Own Horn, Be A Successful Group Member* worksheet.

- Collect the folders and any materials that were distributed. Tell the group members that the next session will be about the importance of paying attention.

I KNOW I CAN

MOTIVATIONAL REMINDER

Session 2: Work Habits
PAY CAREFUL ATTENTION

Objective:

To help students understand why it is important to pay careful attention and to provide opportunities for students to practice paying attention

Materials Needed:

For each student:
- ☑ Student's folder
- ☑ Copy of *Pay Careful Attention* (page 58)
- ☑ Crayons or markers
- ☑ Pencil

For the leader:
- ☑ Timer
- ☑ Collection of several items to use in the *paying attention to what we see* demonstration
- ☑ Smiley face stamp, smiley face stickers, or pencil

Session Preparation:

Reproduce *Pay Careful Attention* for each student. Gather many different items for the demonstration of paying attention to what we see. Gather any other necessary materials.

Session:

- Review the previous session by looking at the laminated train posted on the wall. Read aloud, with the students, the statement: *I Know I Can.*

- Discuss the topic of *paying careful attention.*

  Suggested questions:

  What do the words pay careful attention *mean?*

  How do our bodies show that we are paying attention?

  When should we pay attention?

  Whom should we pay careful attention to at school? At home?

  What keeps us from paying attention?

  Whom do we hurt when we do not pay careful attention?

  How does paying attention help us to do better work at school?

- Tell the students they are going to practice paying careful attention by listening to sounds. Ask the students to listen carefully for one minute to sounds around them. At the end of the minute, ask the students to name the sounds they heard. Discuss the many sounds people can hear if they really pay attention and listen carefully. Repeat the activity. Then ask if the students paid better attention the second time. Encourage the group members to pay careful attention to what they hear in their classrooms.

- Tell the students they are going to practice paying attention to what they see. Show the students a tray containing two or three items. Then ask the students to close their eyes or lower their heads to their desks. Add one item to the tray. Have the students look at the tray and see if they can identify the item that was added. Place several items on the tray. Allow the students to look at the tray for a short time. Ask the students to close their eyes or lower their heads to their desks. Remove one item from the tray. Then have the students look at the tray and see if they can identify the item that you removed. Play different variations of the game. Conclude the game by encouraging the students to pay careful attention to what they see.

- Return each student's folder and distribute *Pay Careful Attention*, a pencil, and crayons or markers to each student. Have the students decorate their worksheets and place them in their folders.

- Continue the lesson by asking:

  Was it difficult to pay attention carefully in this group? Why?

  How do you know you paid attention?

  Is it more difficult to pay attention in your classroom or in this group? Why?

  How do you feel when you pay attention carefully?

  How do you feel when you do not pay attention carefully?

  Which is more difficult—paying careful attention by listening to or by looking at something? Why?

  How can you improve your ability to pay attention carefully?

- Conclude the session asking the students to look at the laminated train posted on the wall and read aloud the words on the completed train cars. Emphasize the importance of paying careful attention.

- Have the students evaluate themselves by deciding whether they took part in the group activities, cooperated with other group members, listened and took turns, and were helpful to the group. Give those students who fulfilled the necessary requirements a smiley face on their *Toot Your Own Horn, Be A Successful Group Member* worksheet.

- Collect the folders and any other materials that were distributed. Tell the group members the next session will be about being a good listener.

PAY CAREFUL
ATTENTION

Session 3: Work Habits
BE A GOOD LISTENER

Objective:

To help students understand the importance of being good listeners and to provide opportunities for group members to practice listening

Materials Needed:

For each student:

- ☑ Student's folder
- ☑ Copy of *Be a Good Listener* (page 62)
- ☑ Crayons or markers
- ☑ Pencil

For the leader:

- ☑ Timer
- ☑ Items for making sounds, such as a bell, paper, whistle, money, wrapped candy
- ☑ Smiley face stamp, smiley face stickers, or pencil

Session Preparation:

Reproduce *Be A Good Listener* for each student. Gather the different items for demonstrating sounds and any other necessary materials.

Session:

- Review the previous session by looking at the laminated train posted on the wall. Read aloud, with the students, the statements: *I Know I Can* and *Pay Careful Attention.*
- Discuss the topic of *being a good listener.*

  Suggested questions:

  What does it mean to be a good listener*?*

  How can you be a good listener?

  Which parts of our bodies do we use when we are good listeners? How is each part used? (Ears hear words, eyes look at the person talking, the brain thinks about what the person is saying.)

  What do you need to be a good listener?

  Who are the people you need to listen carefully to at school? At home? In other places?

  What happens when you do not listen carefully?

  Whom do you hurt when you do not listen carefully?

  How can being a good listener help you do better work in school?

- Teach the group members the acronym BEE to help them remember how to be good listeners. *(BEE = Brain, eyes, ears)*
- Tell the group members they are going to practice being good listeners. Ask the students to close their eyes or lower their heads to their desks while you make mystery sounds. Explain that they will need to listen very carefully to identify the sounds. After making each sound, stop and encourage the group members to identify the sound or identify what made the sound. When the sound is identified, demonstrate how you made the sound.

Suggested sounds:

hum
ring a bell
crumple a piece of paper
write on the chalkboard with chalk
clap your hands
tap a pencil on the table
breathe loudly
tap your shoe on the floor
open and close a door or drawer
blow a whistle
unwrap a piece of candy
rearrange papers
snap your fingers
jingle coins

(*Note:* You may allow the group members take turns making mystery sounds and asking other group members to identify the sounds.)

- Return each the student's folder. Distribute a *Be A Good Listener*, a pencil, and crayons or markers to each student. Have the students practice being good listeners by giving such directions as:

  1. With your pencil, draw a small circle inside each train wheel.
  2. With your black crayon/marker, color the small circles inside the wheels.
  3. Color the outside circles of the wheels with your red crayon/marker.
  4. With your pencil, draw a box around the words *Be A Good Listener.*
  5. Color the box yellow.
  6. Draw three windows in the train car.
  7. In one window, draw a head. (The head or brain represents *thinking about what the speaker is saying.*)
  8. In one window, draw an ear. (The ear represents *listening to the speaker.*)
  9. In one window, draw an eye. (The eye represents *looking at the speaker.*)

- Continue the lesson by asking:

  How did you feel when you were a good listener?

  How do you know you were a good listener?

  How did you feel when you were not a good listener?

  How do you know when you are not a good listener?

  Is it more difficult to be a good listener in this group or in your classroom? Why?

  What can keep you from being a good listener?

- Ask the students to look at the laminated train posted on the wall and read aloud the statements written on the completed train cars. Emphasize the importance of being a good listener.

- Have the students evaluate themselves by thinking about whether they took part in the group activities, cooperated with other group members, listened and took turns, and were helpful to the group. Give those students who fulfilled the necessary requirements a smiley face on their *Toot Your Own Horn, Be A Successful Group Member* worksheet.

- Collect the folders and any other materials that were distributed. Tell the group members the next session will be about following their teacher's directions and rules.

BE A GOOD
LISTENER

BE A GOOD
LISTENER

Session 4: Work Habits

DO WHAT MY TEACHER TELLS ME TO DO

Objective:

To help group members understand the importance of following directions and obeying rules

Session Preparation:

Reproduce *Do What My Teacher Tells Me To Do* for each student. Gather any other necessary materials.

Materials Needed:

For each student:

- ☑ Student's folder
- ☑ Copy of *Do What My Teacher Tells Me To Do* (page 66)
- ☑ Purple, blue, green, orange, and red crayons

For the leader:

- ☑ Smiley face stamp, smiley face stickers, or pencil

Session:

- Review the previous sessions by looking at the laminated train posted on the wall. Read aloud, with the students, the statements: *I Know I Can*, *Pay Careful Attention,* and *Be A Good Listener*.

- Discuss the topic of *Doing What My Teacher Tells Me To Do.*

  Suggested questions:

  > *What does* do what my teacher tells me to do *mean?*
  >
  > *What does* follow directions *mean?*
  >
  > *What does* obey rules *mean?*
  >
  > *How do you make sure you do what your teacher tells you to do?*
  >
  > *How do we make sure we follow directions?*
  >
  > *How do we make sure we obey rules?*
  >
  > *What happens when you do not do what your teacher tells you to do?*
  >
  > *What happens when we do not follow directions?*
  >
  > *What happens when we do not obey rules?*
  >
  > *What are some things that you do that keep you from doing what your teacher tells you to do?*
  >
  > *Whom do you hurt when you do not do what your teacher tells you to do?*
  >
  > *Whom do we hurt when we do not follow directions?*
  >
  > *Whom do we hurt when we do not obey rules?*
  >
  > *What happens when others do not follow directions?*
  >
  > *What happens when others do not obey rules?*
  >
  > *How can doing what your teacher tells you to do help you do better in school?*

- Return each student's folder. Distribute *Do What My Teacher Tells Me To Do* and purple, blue, green, orange, and red crayons to each student.

- Tell the students they must carefully follow directions and obey the rules in order to complete the train cars on their activity sheet.

- State the following rules:

  > *Do not pick up your crayon(s) until I have finished giving each direction.*
  >
  > *You may ask me to repeat a direction if you do not understand what to do. Raise your hand if you need a direction repeated.*

- Give the following directions. Pause after giving each direction to allow time for the students to complete the task.

  1. *Use your purple crayon to write your name inside the small rectangle at the top of the train coal car.*

  2 *On line 1, write these letters to make a word.*

     Write a red F and an orange O.
     Write a blue L and a green L.
     Write a red O and a green W.

3. *On line 2, write these letters to make a word.*

   Write a red D and a blue I.
   Write an orange R and a green E.
   Write a red C and a green T.
   Write an orange I and a blue O
   Write a red N and a green S.

4. *On line 3, write these letters to make a word.*

   Write a red O and a green B.
   Write an orange E and a blue Y.

5. *On line 4, write these letters to make a word.*

   Write a red R and a blue U.
   Write an orange L, a green E, and a red S.

6. *Count the number of words you have written. Use your purple crayon to write that number inside the first wheel.*

7. *Count the number of colors you used on your train. Use your purple crayon to write that number inside the second wheel.*

8. *Count the number of letters in your name. Use your purple crayon to write that number inside the third wheel.*

9. *Count the number of letters in* Do What My Teacher Tells Me To Do. *Use your purple crayon to write that number inside the fourth wheel.*

10. *Take turns reading aloud the words written on the train.*

- Have the students complete the *Do What My Teacher Tells Me To Do* activity sheet by decorating the train cars. Then have them put their activity sheets into their folders.

- Continue the lesson by asking:

  Was it difficult to do what I told you to do?

  Was it difficult to obey rules?

  Was it difficult to follow directions? Why or why not?

  How did you feel when you tried to do what I told you to do?

  Did you have a problem understanding the directions I gave?

  What can you do if you don't understand rules or directions?

  How can you make sure you follow directions?

  How did you feel when you were able to follow the directions I gave?

- Ask the students to look at the laminated train posted on the wall and read aloud the statements written on the completed train cars. Emphasize the importance of doing what the teacher says by following directions and obeying rules.

- Have the students evaluate themselves by thinking about whether they took part in the group activities, cooperated with other group members, listened and took turns, and were helpful to the group. Give those students who fulfilled the necessary requirements a smiley face on their *Toot Your Own Horn, Be A Successful Group Member* worksheet.

- Collect the folders and any other materials that were distributed. Tell the group members the next session will be about working quietly.

1.
2.
3.
4.
DO WHAT
MY TEACHER
TELLS ME TO DO

Session 5: Work Habits
WORK QUIETLY

Objective:

To help students understand the importance of working quietly and to provide opportunities for the group members to practice working quietly

Materials Needed:

For each student:
- ☑ Student's folder
- ☑ Copy of *Work Quietly* (page 70)
- ☑ Green, blue, and yellow crayon

For the leader:
- ☑ Chalkboard and chalk or chart paper and marker
- ☑ Smiley face stamp, smiley face stickers, or pencil

Session Preparation:

Reproduce *Work Quietly* for each student. Gather any other necessary materials.

Session:

- Review the previous sessions by looking at the laminated train posted on the wall. Read aloud, with the students, the statements: *I Know I Can, Pay Careful Attention, Be A Good Listener*, and *Do What My Teacher Tells Me To Do.*
- Discuss the topic of *working quietly.*

Suggested questions:

What does work quietly *mean?*

How do we make sure we work quietly?

When should we work quietly?

What happens when we do not work quietly?

What are some things we do that keep us from working quietly?

Whom do we hurt when we do not work quietly?

What happens when others do not work quietly?

How can working quietly help you do better work in school?

- Return each student's folder. Distribute *Work Quietly* and green, red, blue, and yellow crayons to each student.
- Tell the students there is a secret message on the train car on their activity sheet. To decode the message, they must follow the color key at the bottom of the page.
- Read the color key together:

Color all A's green.
Color all B's red.
Color all C's blue.
Color all other letters yellow.

- While the students work, begin to hum, tap a pencil, or make other noises.
- Observe the students' reactions to your noisy behavior. Do some students become noisy? Do some students continue to work quietly?
- After a couple of minutes, stop the activity and talk about what has happened.
- Write the words *Ignore Distractions* on the board/chart paper. Discuss and demonstrate ignoring. Have the students take turns practicing ignoring distractions when others in the group are noisy.
- Encourage the students to always work quietly and to ignore others who are not working quietly.
- Allow the students to complete the decoding activity. When the students have completed decoding the message, have them read the decoded message aloud.
- Have the students complete their *Work Quietly* activity sheet by decorating the train cars. Then have them put their activity sheet into their folders.
- Ask the students to look at the laminated train posted on the wall and read aloud the statements written on the completed train cars. Emphasize the importance of working quietly.
- Have the students evaluate themselves by thinking about whether they took part in the group activities, cooperated with other group members, listened and took turns, and were helpful to the group. Give those students who fulfilled the necessary requirements a smiley face on their *Toot Your Own Horn, Be A Successful Group Member* worksheet.
- Collect the folders and any other materials that were distributed. Tell the group members the next session will be about personal space and the importance of respecting the space of others.

WORK QUIETLY

WORK QUIETLY
A A A A A A A A A A A A A
A B B B B B B B B B B B A
A B C C W O R K C C C B A
A B C Q U I E T L Y C B A
A B B B B B B B B B B B A
A A A A A A A A A A A A A
FIND THE HIDDEN MESSAGE!
Color all A's green. Color all B's red. Color all C's blue.
Color the other letters yellow.

Session 6: Work Habits
STAY IN MY SPACE

Objective:

To help students understand the concept of personal space, the importance of staying in one's space, and the importance of respecting the space of others

Materials Needed:

For each student:

- ☑ Student's folder
- ☑ Copy of *Stay In My Space* (page 73)
- ☑ Crayons
- ☑ 1 sheet of 18" x 24" construction paper

For the leader:

- ☑ Balloon
- ☑ Smiley face stamp, smiley face stickers, or pencil

Session Preparation:

Reproduce *Stay In My Space* for each student. Gather any other necessary materials.

Session:

- Review the previous sessions by looking at the laminated train posted on the wall. Read aloud, with the students, the statements: *I Know I Can*, *Pay Careful Attention, Be A Good Listener*, *Do What My Teacher Tells Me To Do,* and *Work Quietly.*
- Discuss the topic of *staying in my space.*

Suggested questions:

What is personal space*?*

Why do we need personal space?

Why do others need personal space?

Whose job is it to make sure we stay in our own space?

What can we do if someone gets into our space?

Whom do we hurt if we don't stay in our own space?

What happens when we don't respect others' personal space?

What are some ways we can remember to stay in our own space?

How can staying in your own space help you do better in school?

How can respecting the space of others help you do better in school?

- Play the *Balloon Toss Game.* Place the pieces of construction paper in a circle on the floor. Have the students sit pretzel-style on the construction paper. Tell the students that this is their personal space. Explain that the object of the game is to keep the balloon in motion and not let it drop to the floor. No one may stand up or get off his/her paper to catch the balloon. Toss the balloon into the air. Have the students try to keep the balloon in the air by catching and tossing it when it floats into their space.

Variations of the *Balloon Toss Game*: The game may be played while group members stand on their paper. The balloon may by tapped back into the air, rather than caught and tossed.

- Return each student's folder. Distribute *Stay In My Space* and crayons to each student. Have the students decorate the train car, then place the activity sheet in their folder.

- Continue the lesson by asking:

  Was it difficult to stay in your own space? Why?

  How did you feel when someone got into your space?

  How can you remember to stay in your own space?

  What can you do when you are in line or in some other place where you do not have the personal space you need?

  How can you make sure you don't bother others when your space is small?

  How can you let others know, in a nice way, that they are in your space or are bothering you?

- Ask the students to look at the laminated train posted on the wall and read aloud the statements written on the completed train cars. Emphasize the importance of staying in one's own personal space and respecting the space of others.

- Have the students evaluate themselves by thinking about whether they took part in the group activities, cooperated with other group members, listened and took turns, and were helpful to the group. Give those students who fulfilled the necessary requirements a smiley face on their *Toot Your Own Horn, Be A Successful Group Member* worksheet.

- Collect the folders and any other materials that were distributed. Tell the group members the next session will be about writing neatly.

STAY IN
MY SPACE

Session 7: Work Habits
WRITE NEATLY

Objective:

To help group members understand the importance of writing neatly and to provide opportunities for group members to practice writing neatly

Materials Needed:

For each student:
- ☑ Student's folder
- ☑ Copy of *Write Neatly* (page 76)
- ☑ Pencil
- ☑ Crayons

For the leader:
- ☑ Chalkboard and chalk or chart paper and marker
- ☑ Smiley face stamp, smiley face stickers, or pencil

Session Preparation:

Reproduce *Write Neatly* for each student. Gather any other necessary items.

Session:

- Review the previous sessions by looking at the laminated train posted on the wall. Read aloud, with the students, the statements: *I Know I Can, Pay Careful Attention, Be A Good Listener, Do What My Teacher Tells Me To Do, Work Quietly,* and *Stay In My Space.*
- Discuss the topic of *writing neatly.*

  Suggested questions:

  What do the words write neatly *mean?*

  When do we need to write neatly?

  Why do we need to write neatly?

  What happens if we do not write neatly?

  Who should write neatly?

  What causes us to not write neatly?

  What can we do to help ourselves write more neatly?

  How can writing neatly help you do better work in school?

- Return each student's folder. Distribute *Write Neatly*, crayons, and a pencil to each student.
- Explain that the students should pay attention and listen carefully as you tell them what to write. Then give the following instructions:

  Listen as I call out one letter at a time. The letters will spell two words. Write the letters neatly between the first two lines at the top of the train car.

  First word:

  W R I T E

  Second Word:

  N E A T L Y

- Write *Take your time* on the board/chart paper. Then ask the students to copy the words neatly between the third and fourth lines of their train car.

- Have each student write his/her full name neatly between the fifth and sixth lines of his/her train car.

- Tell the students to decorate their train cars, then put the activity sheet into their folders.

- Check the students' writing for neatness. Then continue the lesson by asking:

  Is it more difficult to write neatly at school or at home? Why?

  How did you feel when you took your time and tried to write neatly?

  How did you feel when you didn't take your time and didn't write neatly?

  How can you learn to write more neatly?

  How do you feel when you can't read someone's writing?

  How do you feel when someone can't read your writing because it isn't neat?

  How do you feel when you hand in a messy paper to your teacher?

  How do you think your teacher feels when he or she sees a messy paper?

- Ask the students to look at the laminated train posted on the wall and read aloud the statements written on the completed train cars. Emphasize the importance of writing neatly all the time.

- Have the students evaluate themselves by thinking about whether they took part in the group activities, cooperated with other group members, listened and took turns, and were helpful to the group. Give those students who fulfilled the necessary requirements a smiley face on their *Toot Your Own Horn, Be A Successful Group Member* worksheet.

- Collect the folders and any other materials that were distributed. Tell the group members the next session will be about doing homework.

WRITE NEATLY

Session 8: Work Habits
DO MY HOMEWORK

Objective:

To help students understand the importance of completing homework and learning to organize homework supplies

Materials Needed:

For each student:

- ☑ Student's folder
- ☑ Copy of *Do My Homework* (page 79)
- ☑ Pencil
- ☑ Crayons

For the leader:

- ☑ Box large enough to hold the supplies
- ☑ Homework supplies (Ruler, pencil, marker, crayons, dictionary, paper, eraser, etc.)
- ☑ Ball
- ☑ Smiley face stamp, smiley face stickers, or pencil

Session Preparation:

Reproduce *Do My Homework* for each student. Gather any other necessary items. Be sure to collect the number of homework supply items equal to the number of students in the group. Place the homework supplies in the box and place the box on a table apart from the students.

Session:

- Review the previous sessions by looking at the laminated train posted on the wall. Read aloud, with the students, the statements: *I Know I Can, Pay Careful Attention, Be A Good Listener, Do What My Teacher Tells Me To Do, Work Quietly, Stay In My Space,* and *Write Neatly.*

- Discuss the topic of *doing homework.*

  Suggested questions:

  What is homework?

  When do teachers assign homework?

  Why do teachers assign homework?

  Why must you do homework when it is assigned?

  Whose job is it to do homework?

  What can you do if you don't understand how to do your homework?

  Whom do you hurt if you don't do your homework?

  What happens when you don't do your homework?

  How can you can remember to do your homework?

  How do you get ready to do your homework?

  Why must you do your best when you do your homework?

  How can always doing your homework help you to do better in school?

- Play the *Ball Toss Game*. Have the students sit in a circle. Show them the homework supplies in the box on the table. Toss the ball to one student. The students who catches the ball selects one item from the table, but does not let the other students know which item he/she selected. The student describes the item, tells how it is used, and why it is important. The other students try to guess what the item is. When someone has guessed what the item is, the student who was describing the item tosses the ball to the person who guessed correctly. The item is then placed back in the box. The process is repeated until each student has had a turn and each homework supply item has been described and identified. Conclude the game by emphasizing the importance of keeping supplies together in a box or in a desk drawer and of having all the supplies needed before beginning homework. Explain that this saves time and makes homework go more smoothly.

- Return each student's folder. Distribute *Do My Homework*, a pencil, and crayons to each student. Have the students fill their train car with drawings of all the supples they need to do their homework. Then have them decorate their train car and put the activity sheet into their folders.

- Continue the lesson by checking the students' writing for neatness, then asking:

  Is it more difficult to complete work at school or at home? Why?

  How did you feel when you completed the assignment of filling your train car with homework supplies?

  What could you do differently to complete the assignment next time?

  How can you get better at finishing your work?

  What must you do to be sure you have all the supplies you need?

- Ask the students to look at the laminated train posted on the wall and read aloud the statements written on the completed train cars. Emphasize the importance of completing homework all the time and having the necessary supplies to complete homework. Emphasize the feelings of accomplishment and self-pride that result from always completing homework.

- Have the students evaluate themselves by thinking about whether they took part in the group activities, cooperated with other group members, listened and took turns, and were helpful to the group. Give those students who fulfilled the necessary requirements a smiley face on their *Toot Your Own Horn, Be A Successful Group Member* worksheet.

- Collect the folders and any other materials that were distributed. Tell the group members the next session will be about taking care of ones things.

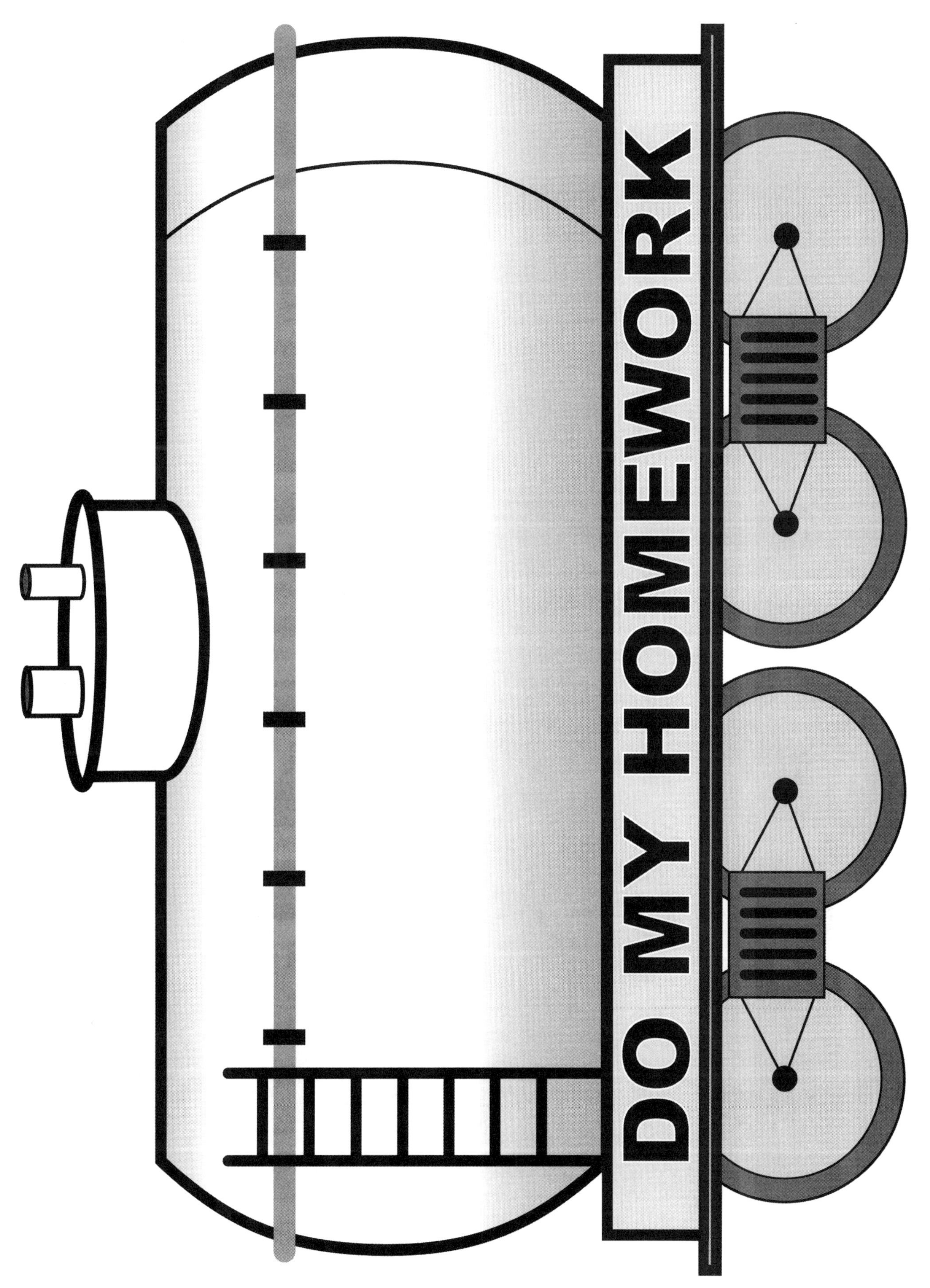
DO MY HOMEWORK

Session 9: Work Habits
TAKE CARE OF MY THINGS

Objective:

To help students understand the importance of always taking care of their things and to think about how well they take care of their things

Materials Needed:

For each student:

- ☑ Student's folder
- ☑ Copy of *Take Care Of My Things* (page 82)
- ☑ Pencil
- ☑ Crayons

For the leader:

- ☑ Chalkboard and chalk or chart paper and marker
- ☑ Smiley face stamp, smiley face stickers, or pencil

Session Preparation:

Reproduce *Take Care Of My Things* for each student. Gather any other necessary items.

Session:

- Review the previous sessions by looking at the laminated train posted on the wall. Read aloud, with the students, the statements: *I Know I Can, Pay Careful Attention, Be A Good Listener, Do What My Teacher Tells Me To Do, Work Quietly, Stay In My Space, Write Neatly,* and *Do My Homework.*

- Discuss the topic of *taking care of one's things.*

  Suggested questions:

  > *What does* take care of my things *mean?*
  >
  > *When do we need to take care of our things?*
  >
  > *Why do we need to take care of our things?*
  >
  > *How does it feel when we know we have taken care of our things?*
  >
  > *What are some ways we don't take care of our things?*
  >
  > *What happens when we don't take care of our things?*
  >
  > *How do your parents/teachers react when you don't take care of your things?*
  >
  > *How can taking good care of your things help you do better work in school?*

- Ask the students to name the different things that must be taken care of in school. Write their answers on the board/chart paper. When the list is complete, talk about how to take care of each item on the list.

- Return each student's folder. Distribute *Take Care Of My Things* and crayons to each student.

- Ask each student to choose three things from the list on the board/chart paper and, in each space on their train car, draw him/herself taking care of one of the items he/she chose. When the students have completed their drawings, have them share their work with the group and discuss it. Tell the students that this picture should help them remember to take care of their things in school.

- Have the students finish decorating their train cars, then place their activity sheet in their folders.

- Continue the lesson by asking:

  > *How do you feel when you take care of your things?*
  >
  > *How do you feel when you don't take care of your things?*
  >
  > *How well do you take care of the things you drew on your train?*
  >
  > *What could you do to take better care of the things you drew?*

- Ask the students to look at the laminated train posted on the wall and read aloud the statements written on the completed train cars. Emphasize the importance of always taking good care of things because it helps them feel good about themselves and do better work in school.

- Have the students evaluate themselves by thinking about whether they took part in the group activities, cooperated with other group members, listened and took turns, and were helpful to the group. Give those students who fulfilled the necessary requirements a smiley face on their *Toot Your Own Horn, Be A Successful Group Member* worksheet.

- Collect the folders and any other materials that were distributed. Tell the group members that the next session will be about always doing one's best.

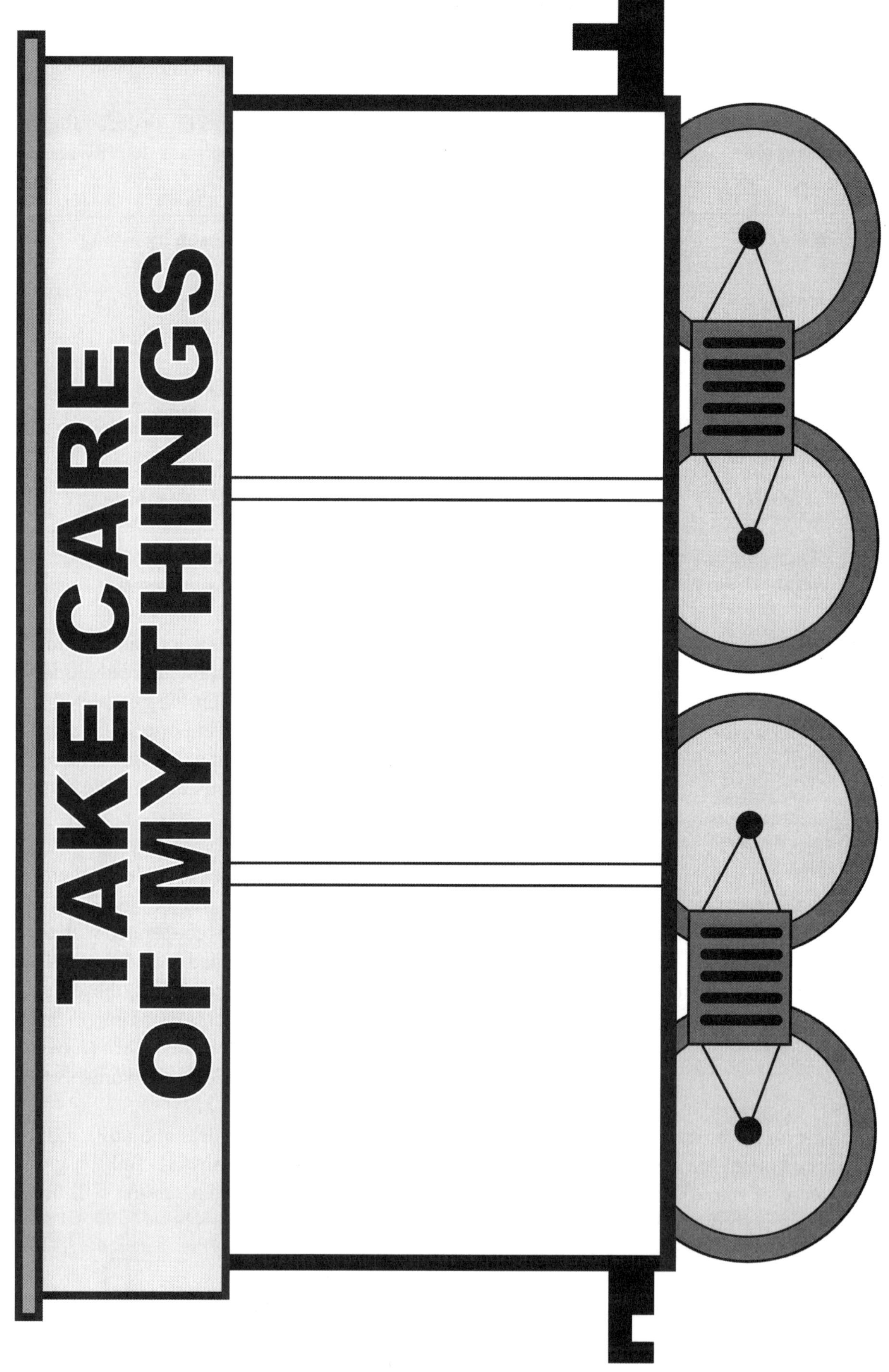
TAKE CARE
OF MY THINGS

Session 10: Work Habits
ALWAYS DO MY BEST

Objective:

To help students understand the importance of always doing one's best and to provide opportunities for group members to practice doing their best

Materials Needed:

For each student:

- ☑ Student's folder
- ☑ Copy of *Always Do My Best* (page 85)
- ☑ Sheet of 12" x 18" drawing paper
- ☑ Pencil
- ☑ Crayons or markers

For the leader:

- ☑ Smiley face stamp, smiley face stickers, or pencil

Session Preparation:

Reproduce *Always Do My Best* for each student. Gather any other necessary items.

Session:

- Review the previous sessions by looking at the laminated train posted on the wall. Read aloud, with the students, the statements: *I Know I Can, Pay Careful Attention, Be A Good Listener, Do What My Teacher Tells Me To Do, Work Quietly, Stay In My Space, Write Neatly, Do My Homework,* and *Take Care Of My Things.*

- Discuss the topic of *always doing one's best.*

  Suggested questions:

  What does do my best *mean?*

  When do we need to try hard to do our best?

  Why do we need to do our best? (Emphasize self-pride.)

  How does it feel when we know we have tried hard and done our very best?

  What are some ways we avoid trying hard? Doing our best? Giving our best effort?

  How do our parents/teacher react when we do our best?

  How do our parents/teacher react when we do not do our best?

  How can giving your best effort and doing your best help you do better work in school?

- Involve the students in completing a group picture. Explain that they are going to work together to draw a train's passenger car. Each person will be responsible for doing his/her best. As the drawing is passed from person to person, each student will draw a certain part of the car. In order to do this, each student must listen and carefully follow the instructions you give. After each person draws, the train car drawing is passed to the next person. There should be enough directions so that every group member draws a portion of the train car.

- Distribute a piece of drawing paper, a pencil, and crayons or markers to each student. The students may use their crayons or pencils or both. Then give the following instructions. (*Note:* Depending on the number of students in the group, you may need to combine instructions so the number of instructions equals the number of students in the group.) Pause after giving each instruction for the students to complete the task.

    1. Draw a large rectangle. Be sure the rectangle is large enough so you can add many passengers to the car.

    2. Draw two front wheels.

    3. Draw two back wheels.

    4. Draw a train track under the wheels of the passenger car.

    5. Draw a door in the center of the car.

    6. Draw steps leading up to the door.

    7. Draw a window for each group member.

    8. If necessary, give additional directions so that each group member has a turn to draw.

    The completed drawing should be returned to the person who completed Instruction #1.

- Optional Activity: Pass the train around a second time. Ask each student to draw him/herself as a passenger looking out one of the windows.

    If the students are only using pencils, pass the drawing around again for cooperative coloring.

- Continue the lesson by asking:

    Was it difficult for you to add to someone else's work? Why or why not?

    Why was it important to try very hard to do your best work?

    Why was it important to pay attention, listen carefully, and work quietly as you added to the drawing?

    How did you feel when we all worked together and did our best?

    How do you feel now that your group drawing is completed?

- Ask the students to look at the laminated train posted on the wall and read aloud the statements written on the completed train cars. Emphasize the importance of always trying to do one's best. Explain that this is important because doing one's best helps us feel good about ourselves.

- Return each student's folder. Distribute *Do My Best* to each student. Have the students draw a picture of themselves in the space where the bricks are, decorate their worksheets, and place them in their folders.

- Have the students evaluate themselves by thinking about whether they took part in the group activities, cooperated with other group members, listened and took turns, and were helpful to the group. Give those students who fulfilled the necessary requirements a smiley face on their *Toot Your Own Horn, Be A Successful Group Member* worksheet.

- Collect the folders and any other materials that were distributed. Tell the group members the next session will be about being responsible.

DO
MY
BEST

Session 11: Work Habits
FINAL SESSION—BE RESPONSIBLE

Objective:

To help students understand the importance of being responsible in school, to encourage them to accept responsibility and use good study skills and work habits, and to assess how responsible each group member is being

Materials Needed:

For each student:

- ☑ Student's foldcr
- ☑ Copy of *I Know I Can Be Responsible* (page 88)
- ☑ Pencil
- ☑ Crayons
- ☑ Copy of *Be Responsible* (page 89)
- ☑ Notecard-size *Train Cars* (optional, pages 90-92)
- ☑ Copy of *Super Engineer* (optional, page 93)

For the leader:

- ☑ Smiley face stamp, smiley face stickers, or pencil
- ☑ Tape (optional)

Session Preparation:

Reproduce *I Know I Can Be Responsible* and *Be Responsible* for each student. Gather any other necessary items. Optional: Reproduce the notecard-size *Train Cars* and *Super Engineer* awards.

Session:

- Review the previous sessions by looking at the laminated train posted on the wall. Read aloud, with the students, the statements: *I Know I Can, Pay Careful Attention, Be A Good Listener, Do What My Teacher Tells Me To Do, Work Quietly, Stay In My Space, Write Neatly, Do My Homework, Take Care Of My Things,* and *Always Do Your Best.*

- Discuss the topic of *being responsible.*

  Suggested questions:

  What does it mean to be responsible*?*

  When do we need to be responsible?

  Why do we need to be responsible?

  How does it feel to act responsibly?

  What are some ways we try to avoid being responsible?

  If we are responsible in school, will we always get all the right answers and have everything turn out perfectly? (Emphasize that there are times when we cannot be completely successful or do things perfectly.)

  What are some of the reasons we make mistakes? (Emphasize that it is OK to make a mistake as long as we are trying our best and learn from our mistakes.)

  Who can be hurt if we are not responsible?

What are some things that cause us not to act responsibly?

How can being responsible help you do better in school?

What is the most important thing about being responsible in school? (giving our best effort)

- Distribute the *I Know I Can Be Responsible* self-evaluation checklist and a pencil to each student. Tell the students that you will read each statement aloud. Challenge the students to honestly assess their study skills and work habits.

- Return each student's folder. Distribute *Be Responsible* and crayons to each student. Have the students decorate the final car, then place it in their folders.

Optional Follow-Up:

- Distribute tape and the train-car notecards reflecting areas needing improvement to students who need improvement in those areas. Have the students tape these cards to their desks to remind them to "get on track" by continuing to think about and work to improve their study skills and work habits.

- Continue the lesson by asking:

Is it more difficult to be responsible at home or at school? Why?

How can we become more responsible?

- Explain that students who marked "sometimes" and "no" on the checklist, need to continue to work on improving their study skills and work habits.

- Encourage the group members to become more responsible by keeping their checklists and trying to improve the skills not marked with a smiley face.

- Ask the students to look at the laminated train posted on the wall and read aloud the statements written on the completed train cars. Emphasize that being responsible means always trying to do one's best. Tell the students to try to use each skill listed on each train car. Remind the students that using these skills and practicing these good habits helps them learn to be more responsible and become better students.

- Have the students evaluate themselves by thinking about whether they took part in the group activities, cooperated with other group members, listened and took turns, and were helpful to the group. Give those students who fulfilled the necessary requirements a smiley face on their *Toot Your Own Horn, Be A Successful Group Member* worksheet.

- Optional: Distribute the *Super Engineer* awards to the group members.

- Have the students take their folders, evaluation forms, and completed trains with them. Collect any materials that were distributed.

I KNOW I CAN BE RESPONSIBLE

Name____________________________________ Date____________________

Put "X" in the square that best describes you!

I KNOW I CAN

		YES	SOMETIMES	NO
1.	I pay attention carefully in school.	☐	☐	☐
2.	I am a good listener in school.	☐	☐	☐
3.	I do what my teacher tells me to do.	☐	☐	☐
4.	I work quietly in school.	☐	☐	☐
5.	I stay in my own space.	☐	☐	☐
6.	I do my homework.	☐	☐	☐
7.	I write neatly in school.	☐	☐	☐
8.	I take care of my things.	☐	☐	☐
9.	I do my best in school.	☐	☐	☐
10.	I am responsible in school.	☐	☐	☐

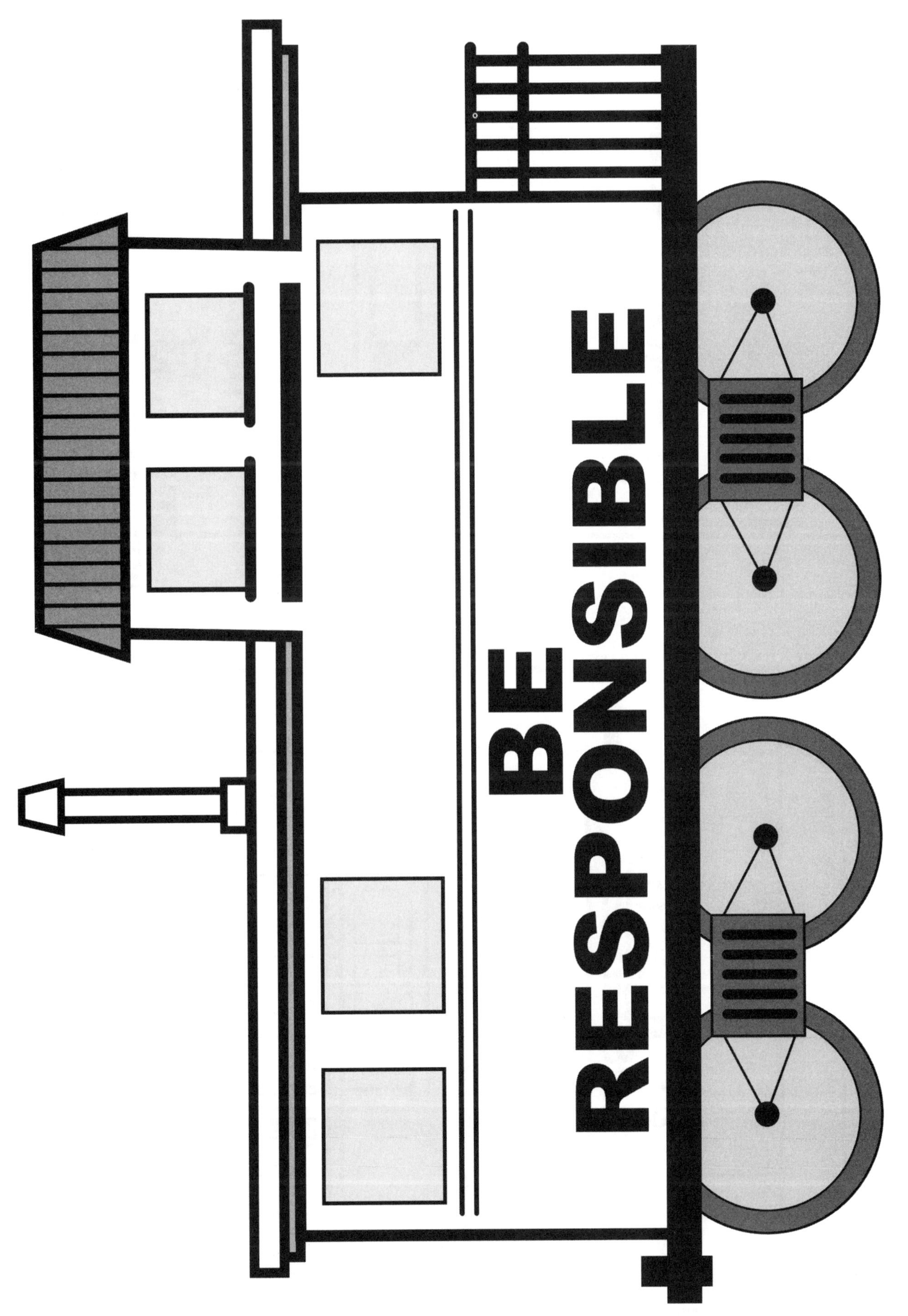
BE
RESPONSIBLE

NOTE CARDS

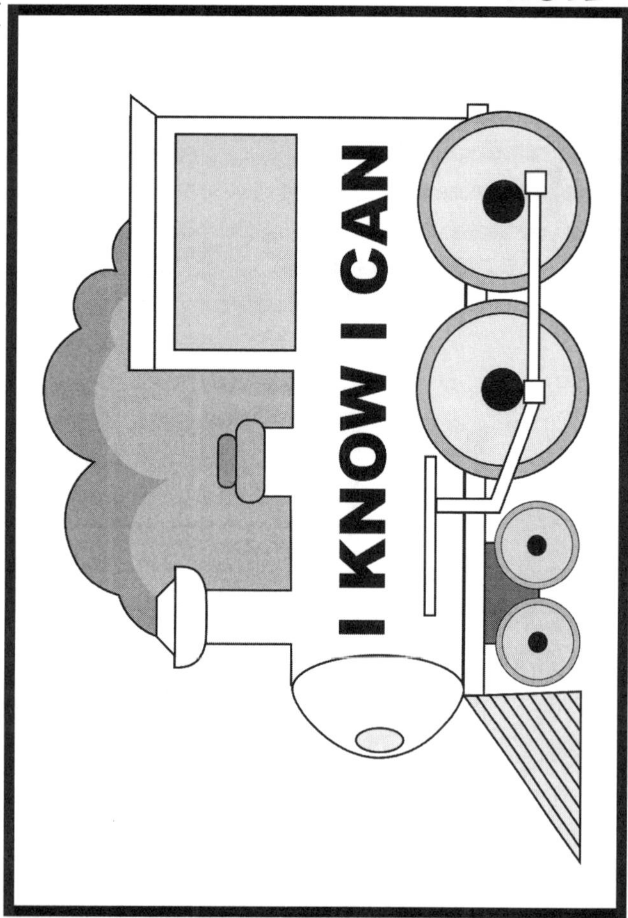
I KNOW I CAN

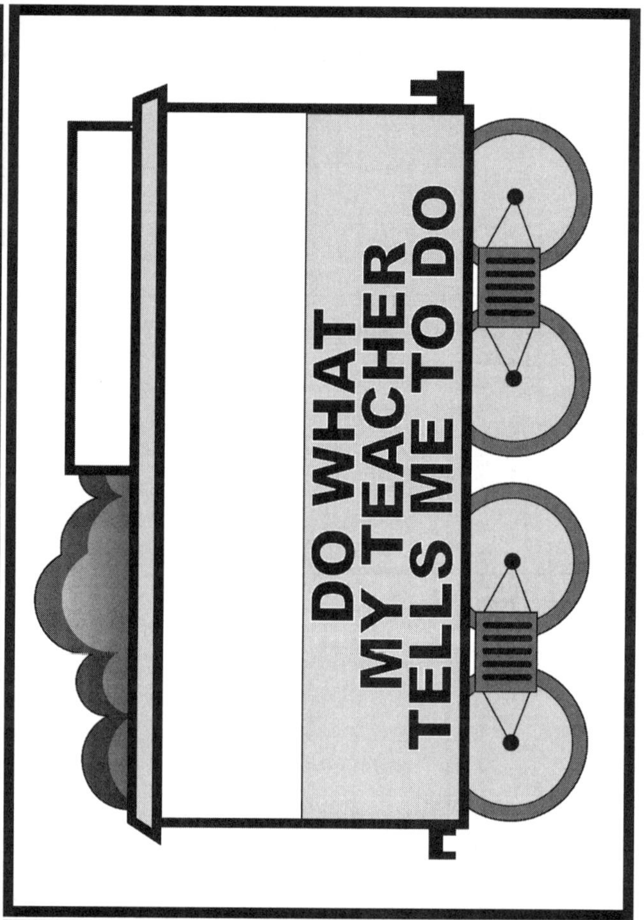
DO WHAT
MY TEACHER
TELLS ME TO DO

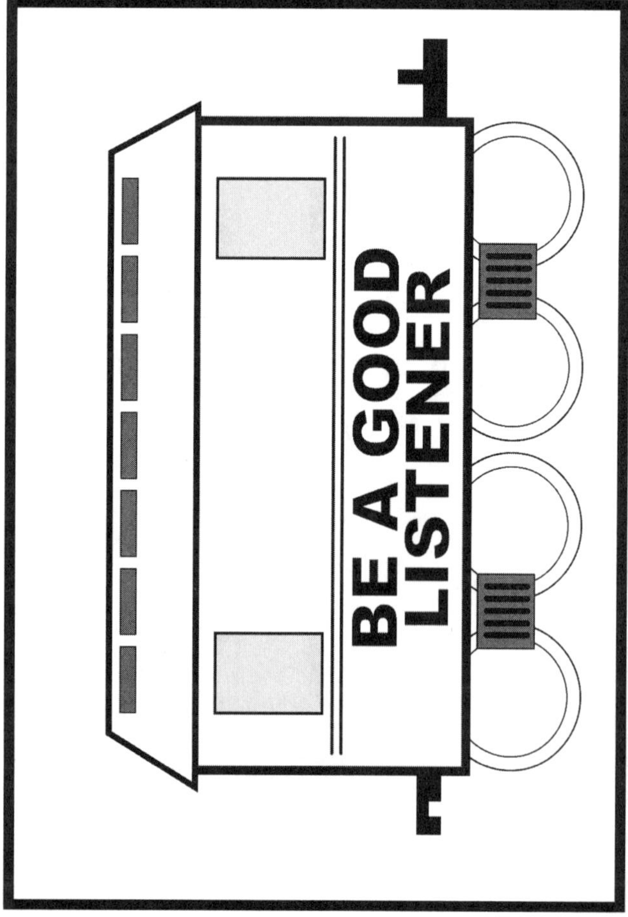
BE A GOOD
LISTENER

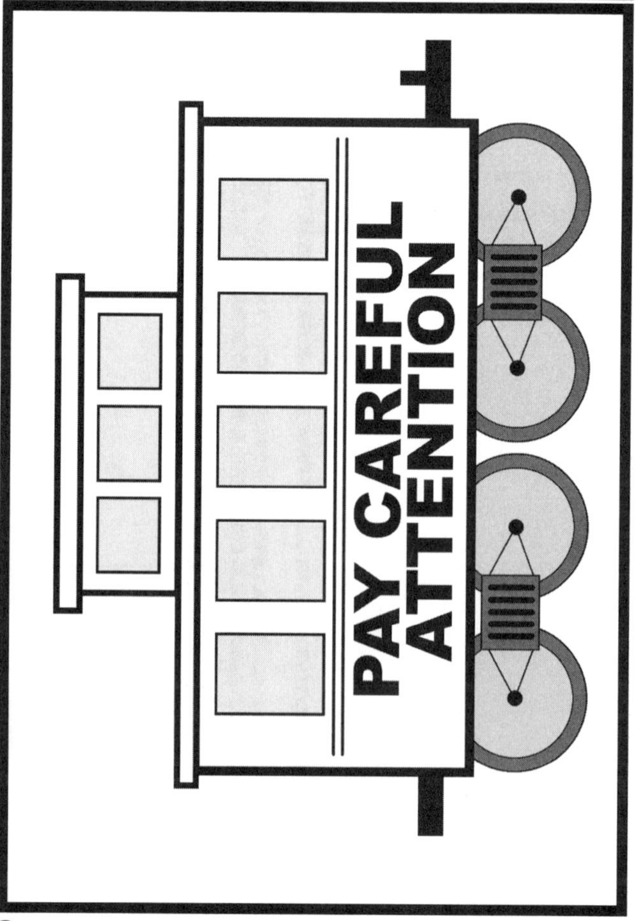
PAY CAREFUL
ATTENTION

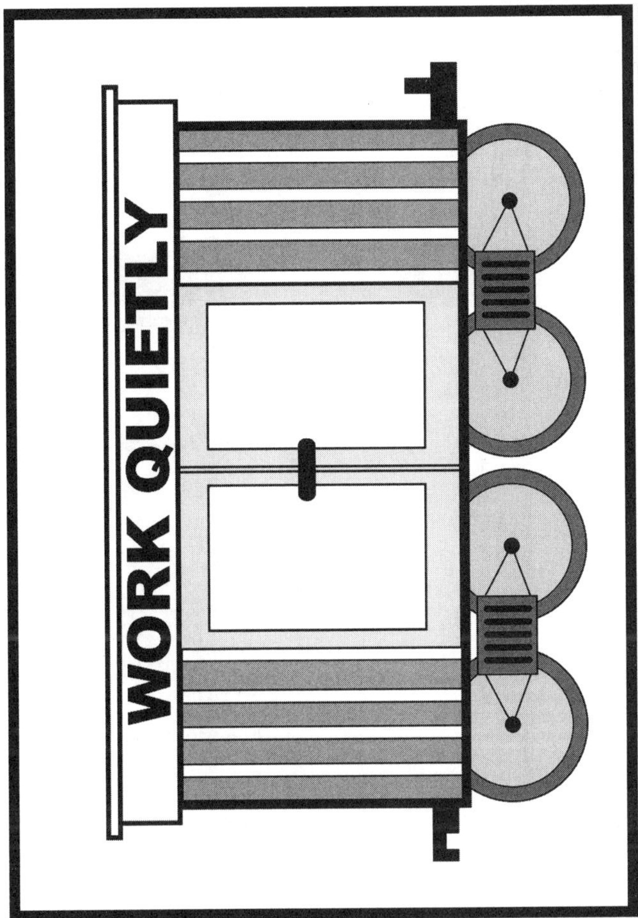

NOTE CARDS

WORK QUIETLY

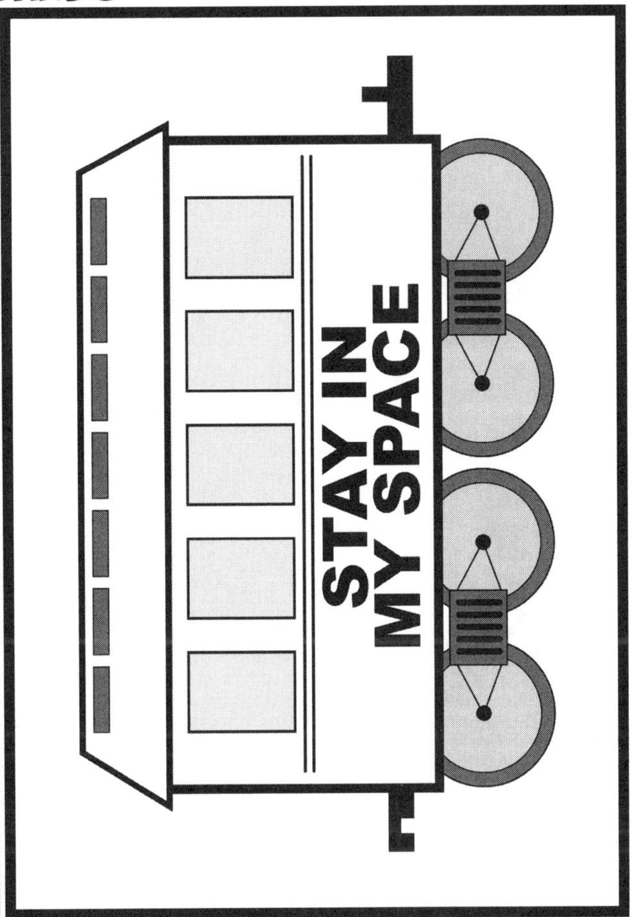

STAY IN
MY SPACE

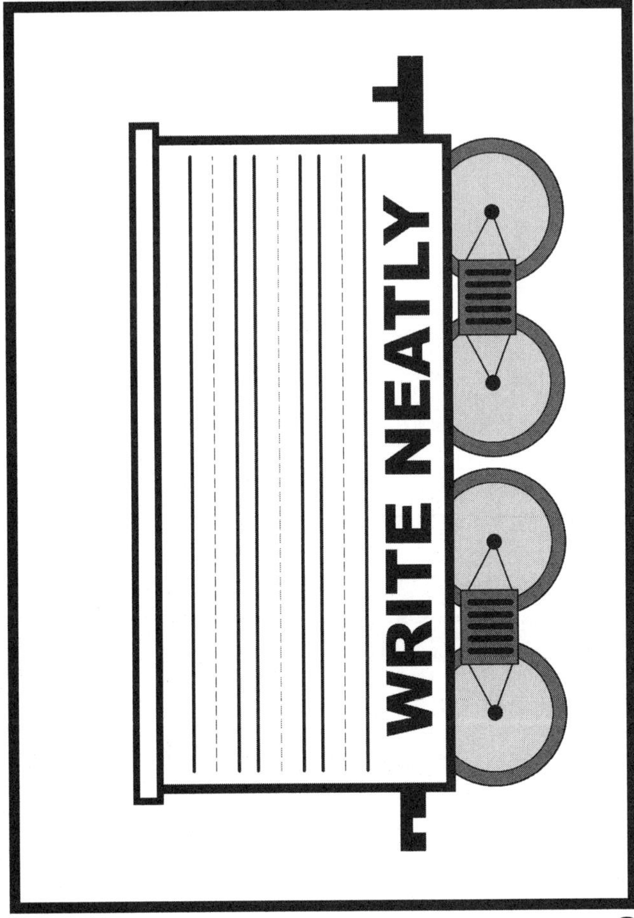

WRITE NEATLY

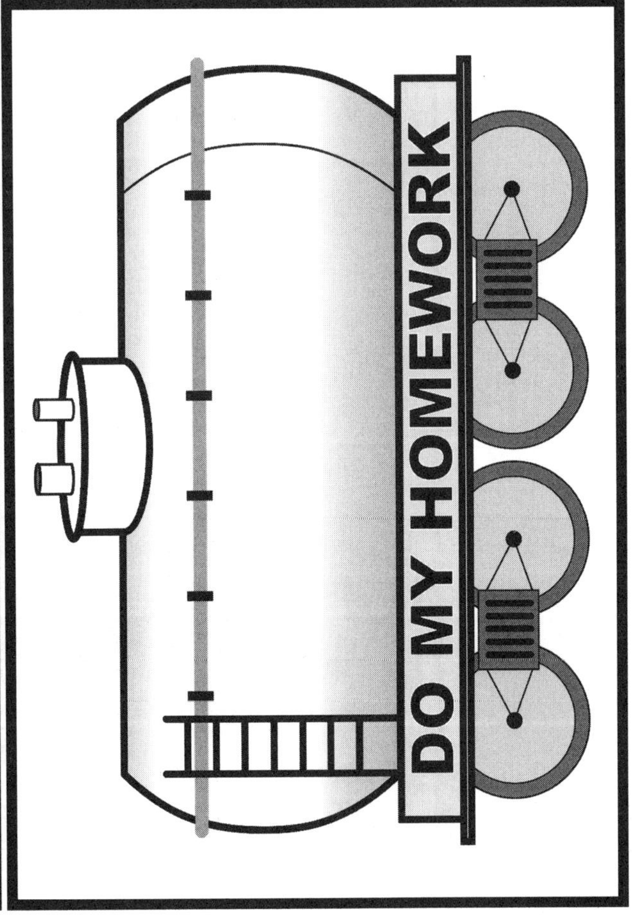

DO MY HOMEWORK

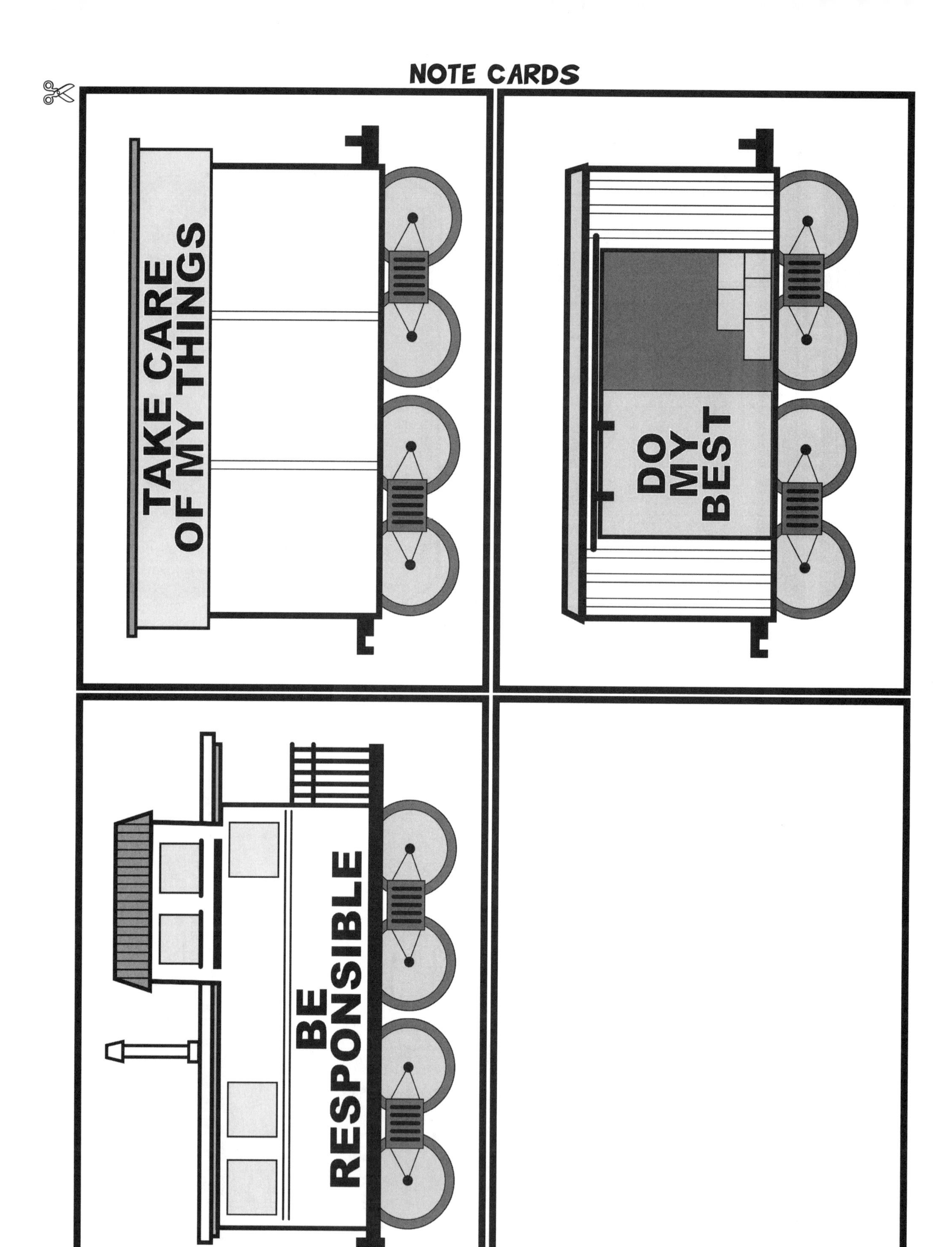
TAKE CARE
OF MY THINGS
DO
MY
BEST
BE
RESPONSIBLE

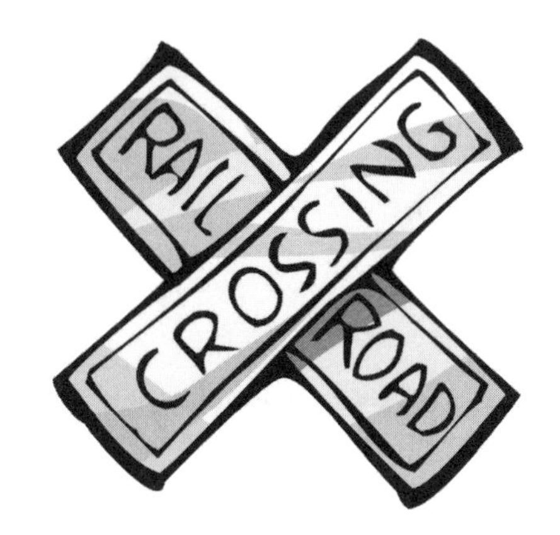

SUPER ENGINEER

★ ★ ★ ★ ★ ★

____

IS NOW ON TRACK AND ALL ABOARD THE STUDY SKILLS/ WORK HABITS EXPRESS!

GOOD WORK!

MAKING THE DECISION TO LEARN

(Positive Attitudes = Academic Improvement—Grades 1-3)

Attitudes toward learning are established at an early age as a result of school experiences and parental attitudes. Students who have a positive attitude achieve more. Those with a negative attitude develop behaviors that stifle their learning potential.

Each session in this six-session group is approximately 30 minutes long. The group does require parental input. After each session, students will take home a paper that requires parents and children to work together for about 15 minutes. Those papers are brought to the next session and placed in each student's folder.

This group is designed to help students:

- Realize the importance of school
- Establish regular one-on-one time to discuss the importance of school with their parents

Group candidates:

- Students who do not take school seriously
- Students who seem apprehensive about the importance of school
- Six to eight students from the same or adjoining grade levels

Group preparation:

Interview each student selected individually and explain why the group is forming and how it will work. Then send a parental notification and permission letter (page 95) home with each student selected to be a group member.

Dear ____:

The importance of a good attitude toward school cannot be too strongly emphasized. Students who have a positive attitude achieve more than those who have a negative attitude. Negative attitudes toward school may be acquired at an early age and, if not reversed, can hinder a child throughout his or her school years. Attitudes come from obvious sources, like older peers influencing younger students, and from less-obvious sources, such as casual statements that are taken more seriously than intended.

Every young child deserves the best a school has to offer. That is why it is important for every child to have an attitude that promotes success. Your child's classroom teacher has identified your child as a student who could use extra help with understanding the importance of school.

In an effort to help your child and others, I am forming a counseling group that will focus on helping students grasp this important concept. Our group will emphasize ways that learning helps students play, identify interesting things they have learned in school, talk about things they would like to learn, and discuss their responsibility for their own learning.

The six group meetings will each be approximately 30-minutes long. They will be held at a time the classroom teacher selects.

Your child knows about the group and has indicated that he or she would like to participate in it. However, no child is ever included in a small-group counseling program without his or her parents' knowledge and permission.

Please indicate, by completing the form below, that you wish to have your child participate in this group or that you do not want him or her to be included.

Return the permission slip to me by ____________________________.

Thank you,

✂- -

☐ I, ____________________________________, ***give permission*** for my child to participate in the small-group counseling program focusing on the importance of school in his or her life.

☐ I, ____________________________________, ***do not give permission*** for my child to participate in the small-group counseling program focusing on the importance of school in his or her life.

Child's Name ____________________________________ Date ______________

School ____________________________________ Grade ______________

Teacher ____________________________________

Home Phone (_____) ________________ Work Phone (_____) ______________

Parent's Printed Name ____________________________________

Parent's Signature ____________________________________

Session 1: Positive Attitude
INTRODUCTION

Objective:

To explain the group's purpose and parents' role in the group, and to elicit each student's impression of school

Materials Needed:

For each student:

- ☑ Sheet of 12" x 18" drawing paper
- ☑ Pencil
- ☑ Crayons
- ☑ Sheet of lined paper
- ☑ Copy of *Dear_______,* (optional, page 97)

For the leader:

- ☑ Chalkboard and chalk or chart paper and marker

Session Preparation:

Gather the necessary materials. Give each student a copy of *Dear_______,* or write the following on the board:

> Dear (PARENTS' NAME),
>
> I will be meeting six times with our guidance counselor, (COUNSELOR'S NAME). I will be learning about the importance of school. I will need your help. Each time we meet, I will be doing something that shows how home and school work together. I would like to work with you on this.
>
> Your (SON OR DAUGHTER),
> (NAME OF STUDENT)
>
> I will work with my child to help (HIM OR HER) learn about the importance of school.
>
> (PARENT'S SIGNATURE)

Session:

- Have each student introduce him/herself and state one word that reminds him/her of school.
- Distribute drawing paper, a pencil, and crayons to each student. Tell the students to fold the paper in half lengthwise, then unfold it. On the right side of the fold, have the students draw a picture of school. When the students have completed drawing the school, tell them to draw themselves somewhere in the picture.
- Collect the completed pictures. Allow those students who wish to do so to say something about their pictures.
- Tell the students that after each session, they will be doing something at home with their parents. Explain that their parents are aware of this.
- Distribute a piece of lined paper to each student. Tell the students to look at the board and copy the letter to their parents. Or distribute *Dear_______,* to each student. Tell the students how to fill in the letter.
- Instruct the students to take the letter home, have their parents sign it, and bring it to the next session.
- Have the students fold their paper so the drawing of the school will become a cover, then put their names on the cover. Explain that these folders will hold all the activity sheets they complete in the group. The letter they are taking home to be signed will be the first paper to go into their folders.
- Collect the pictures and any materials that were distributed.

Dear________________________________,

I will be meeting six times with our guidance counselor, ________________________________. I will be learning about the importance of school. I will need your help. Each time we meet, I will be doing something that shows how home and school work together. I would like to work with you on this.

Your_________________________,

____

YOUR NAME

I will work with my child to help him/her learn about the importance of school.

____

PARENT'S SIGNATURE

Session 2: Positive Attitude
LEARNING HELPS US PLAY

Objective:

To show students that they need basic school skills to enjoy the games they play

Materials Needed:

For each student:

- ☑ Student's folder
- ☑ Copy of *Learning Sheet #1* (page 99)
- ☑ Pencil

For the leader:

- ☑ Timer
- ☑ Chalkboard and chalk or chart paper and marker
- ☑ Two or three commercial games that require students to count or read

Session Preparation:

Reproduce *Learning Sheet #1* for each student. Gather the other needed materials.

Session:

- Distribute the folders and have the students place their signed letters in them. Collect the folders.
- Divide the students into two or three small groups.
- Give each group a game. Tell the students they may play their game for 10 minutes. When the allotted time has elapsed, have one student from each group put the game away.
- Ask the students to name all the subjects they study in school. Record the students' answers on the board/chart paper.
- Then ask the students to think about how subjects they study in school helped them play the games. (Look for answers such as, "Math helps me learn to count" and "Without reading, I could not read the directions or other words in the game.")
- Continue the discussion until the students realize that school helps them learn to play.
- Distribute *Learning Sheet #1* and a pencil to each student.
- Have the students think of five games they enjoy at home or in school. Ask them to list the names of the games on the lines below the *Games* column.
- Have the students think of school subjects that help them play these games, then write one subject for each game on the lines below the *Subjects* column.
- Tell the students to take *Learning Sheet #1* home and sit down with a parent for about 15 minutes. Have the students show their parents the paper, then ask their parents to think of five games they enjoyed as children. Either the parent or the child may write the names of those games on the lines provided. Then the child and the parent should answer the questions at the bottom of the page. The completed paper should be brought to the next session.

Learning Sheet #1
LEARNING HELPS US PLAY

Name______________________________ Date__________________

Think about five games you play at school or at home. Write the names of these games on the lines in *Games* column. Then think of which subjects you study in school that help you play each game. Write the name of the subject in the *Subjects* column.

GAMES	SUBJECTS
1. ________________	________________
2. ________________	________________
3. ________________	________________
4. ________________	________________
5. ________________	________________

Parent/Child Activity: Do you know what games your parent enjoyed as a child? Spend a few minutes to ask your parent what games were important to him/her as a child. Write the names of these games on the following lines. Then answer the questions at the bottom of the page.

1. ______________________________
2. ______________________________
3. ______________________________
4. ______________________________
5. ______________________________

1. Are any of the games you listed the same as ones your parent listed? ________________
2. What school subjects would your parent have to know in order to play the games on his/her list?

   ____

   ____
3. Would you like to learn any of the games on your parent's list? ________________

Session 3: Positive Attitude

INTERESTING THINGS I HAVE LEARNED IN SCHOOL

Objective:

To have the students identify interesting things they have learned each year in school

Materials Needed:

For each student:

☑ Student's folder
☑ Copy of *Learning Sheet #2* (Select the activity sheet appropriate for the grade level with which you are working—pages 102-104)
☑ Pencil

For the leader:

☑ Chalkboard and chalk or chart paper and marker

Session Preparation:

Reproduce the appropriate copy of *Learning Sheet #2*. Gather the other needed materials.

Session:

- Distribute the students' folders.
- Check to see that each student has completed *Learning Sheet #1*. Then have the students put the activity sheet into their folders. Collect the folders.
- Ask the students the meaning of the word *interesting*. (Something that holds your attention.)
- Have the students name some things that are interesting to them.
- Tell the students you are going to name two things, then designate a spot in the room for each thing. Explain that the students should choose the thing that is most interesting to them, then move to that thing's designated area. Give the students time to move to their spots. After one or two students move to each area, have the students tell why they made that choice. Begin the activity by asking:

  Are you more interested in reading a book or writing a story?

  Are you more interested in drawing a picture or playing a game with a friend?

  Are you more interested in working math problems or doing a science experiment?

  Are you more interested in learning about birds or being in a play?

  Are you more interested in working with a group or working by yourself?

- Ask the students to think about all the years they have been in school. Tell them this is like a trip back in time. They are to remember one interesting thing they learned in each grade. Begin with kindergarten, asking the students to tell one interesting thing they learned that year. Continue with each completed grade, including the students' current grade.
- Distribute *Learning Sheet #2* and a pencil to each student. Have the students complete their drawings or the sentences on the activity sheet.

- Review the activity the students will complete with their parents. Tell them to set time aside to work with their parents. During this time, the parents will talk about what their school days were like. Encourage the students to ask questions about their parents' school days. (*Note:* To give more specific directions, you may ask the students for examples of questions they could ask their parents.)

- Review, with the students, the questions to be answered by their parents. Tell the students to return their completed activity sheets at the next session.

- Collect the students' folders and any materials that were distributed.

Learning Sheet #2

INTERESTING THINGS I HAVE LEARNED IN SCHOOL

Name______________________________________ Date___________________

Think about what you have learned in school. You have learned many things each year. First think about what you learned in kindergarten and what was most interesting for you. Draw a picture of what was most interesting to you.

Crayon

Think about this year. What is the most interesting thing you have learned about in first grade? Draw a picture of what was most interesting to you.

Crayon

Parent/Child Activity: Spend a few minutes talking with your parent about what interesting things he/she did in school. Then work together to complete the following statements.

An interesting book I read as a child was ____ .

My favorite subject in school was ____ .

One project I did as a child was ____ .

My most interesting teacher was ____ .

Learning Sheet #2

INTERESTING THINGS I HAVE LEARNED IN SCHOOL

Name ______________________________ Date ________________

Think about what you have learned in school. You have learned many things each year. During each year you have learned many things. Can you remember some of the things you have learned? Now think about some of the things your teachers have taught you during each year. Decide what was the most interesting thing you learned for each year you have been in school.

The most interesting thing I learned in Kindergarten was ______________________________

____

____.

The most interesting thing I learned in Grade 1 was ______________________________

____

____.

The most interesting thing I learned in Grade 2 was ______________________________

____

____.

Parent/Child Activity: Spend a few minutes talking with your parent about what interesting things he/she did in school. Then work together to complete the following statements.

An interesting book I read as a child was ______________________________.

My favorite subject in school was ______________________________.

One project I did as a child was ______________________________.

My most interesting teacher was ______________________________.

Learning Sheet #2

INTERESTING THINGS I HAVE LEARNED IN SCHOOL

Name ______________________________ Date ________________

Think about what you have learned in school. You have learned many things each year. During each year you have learned many things. Can you remember some of the things you have learned? Now think about some of the things your teachers have taught you during each year. Decide what was the most interesting thing you learned for each year you have been in school.

The most interesting thing I learned in Kindergarten was ______________________

____

____.

The most interesting thing I learned in Grade 1 was ______________________

____

____.

The most interesting thing I learned in Grade 2 was ______________________

____

____.

The most interesting thing I learned in Grade 3 was ______________________

____

____.

Parent/Child Activity: Spend a few minutes talking with your parent about what interesting things he/she did in school. Then work together to complete the following statements.

An interesting book I read as a child was ______________________________.

My favorite subject in school was ______________________________.

One project I did as a child was ______________________________.

My most interesting teacher was ______________________________.

Session 4: Positive Attitude
THINGS I WOULD LIKE TO LEARN

Objective:

To have students identify things they have learned in different subjects since they began school and choose something they would still like to learn about each subject

Materials Needed:

For each student:
- ☑ Student's folder
- ☑ Copy of *Learning Sheet #3* (page 106)
- ☑ Pencil

For the leader:
- ☑ Chalkboard and chalk or chart paper and marker
- ☑ Yardstick, pointer (optional)

Session Preparation:

Reproduce *Learning Sheet #3* for each student. Gather the other needed materials.

Session:

- Distribute the students' folders.
- Check to see that each student has completed *Learning Sheet #2.* Then have the students put the activity sheet into their folders. Collect the folders.
- Distribute *Learning Sheet #3* and a pencil to each student.
- Tell the students you are going to name different subjects they study in school and that you want them to tell you what they have learned in each subject.
- Have the students stand. Then ask:

  What have you learned in math since you started school?

  When a student responds to the question, he/she may sit down. Record the students' responses on the board/chart paper.
- Using your *magic wand* (yardstick, pointer, or your hand), turn one student into the *Most Powerful Person In The Group*. Explain that this person may grant or deny the wishes of other group members.
- Tell the students to think about what they would still like to learn in math.
- Have them ask the *Most Powerful Person In The Group* for permission to learn it.
- If the *Most Powerful Person In The Group* does not grant the wish, he/she must explain why.
- Have each student make a wish.
- Tell the students to complete the sentence *One thing I would like to learn in math is ...* on their *Learning Sheet.*
- Choose a different student to be the *Most Powerful Person In The Group.* Continue the game, choosing a new person after each subject is completed, until each subject on *Learning Sheet #3* has been discussed and the sentences have all been completed.
- Explain the week's *Parent/Child Activity* and tell the students to return their sheets at the next session.
- Collect the students' folders and any materials that were distributed.

Learning Sheet #3
THINGS I WOULD LIKE TO LEARN

Name ______________________________ Date______________

Imagine you have the power to learn anything you like. What would you want to learn? Think about the subjects below and pick one thing you would like to know that you do not know already.

One thing I would like to learn in math is ____

____ .

One thing I would like to learn in science is ______________________________________

____ .

In art, I would like to learn ____

____ .

In gym, I would like to learn ____

____ .

One word I would like to learn to spell is____ .

In reading, I would like to learn to ____

____ .

In social studies, I would like to learn about ______________________________________

____ .

Parent/Child Activity: Learning does not end when you finish school. Learning goes on forever. Spend some time and talk with your parent about things he/she has learned since finishing school and things he/she would still like to learn. Write down what your parent tells you about the following statements. Remember that your answers do not have to be related to school. They can be anything at all.

One thing I learned to do since I finished school was ____________________________ .

I learned it by ____ .

One thing I would still like to learn to do is ____ .

Someday I would like to read a book about ____ .

Session 5: Positive Attitude

RESPECT MY SCHOOL

Objective:

To have the students identify the meaning of the word *respect* and discuss what school would be like if it were not respected and how to show respect in school

Materials Needed:

For each student:

- ☑ Student's folder
- ☑ Copy of *Learning Sheet #4* (page 108)
- ☑ Pencil

For the leader:

- ☑ Chalkboard and chalk or chart paper and marker

Session Preparation:

Reproduce *Learning Sheet #4* for each student. Gather the other needed materials.

Session:

- Distribute the students' folders.
- Check to see that each student has completed *Learning Sheet #3*. Then have the students put the activity sheet into their folders. Collect the folders.
- Have the students define the word *respect*. (Continue eliciting responses from the students until it is clear that *respect* means *showing consideration for something or someone.*)
- On the board/chart paper, draw an outline of a school.
- Ask the students what school would be like if they did not respect it.
- Have different students come to the board/chart paper and add to the picture by illustrating objects that make the school look disrespected (broken windows, trash in the yard, etc.).
- Distribute *Learning Sheet #4* and a pencil to each student.
- Tell the students they are going to take an imaginary trip around their school.
- Pretend to visit, with the students, each place mentioned on the *Learning Sheet.* When you arrive at each place, have the students describe what it would look like if people did not respect the school and how the people in that place would be treated if the students did not respect them. (Students would be rude to the secretary in the school office, run and make noise in the halls, leave the cafeteria littered with food and papers, etc.)
- Ask the students to think of one way they could show respect in each place mentioned on their *Learning Sheet.* Tell them to write their answers in the spaces provided.
- Explain the week's *Parent/Child Activity* and tell the students this will be the last activity they will be doing with their parents. Tell them to return their sheets at the next session.
- Collect the students' folders and any materials that were distributed.

Learning Sheet #4
I RESPECT MY SCHOOL

Name______________________________ Date__________________

Respect means to ***show consideration for something or someone***. We are going to take an imaginary trip around our school and name ways we can show respect for the people in our building and for school property.

THE SCHOOL OFFICE

____

____

____

THE CAFETERIA

____

____

____

THE HALLS

____

____

____

THE SCHOOLYARD

____

____

____

THE CLASSROOM

____

____

____

Parent/Child Activity: Ask your parent to name some things he/she likes about your school. Write your parent's answers on the lines below.

____

____

____

Session 6: Positive Attitude
CONCLUSION

Objective:

To help students realize the importance of learning

Materials Needed:

For each student:
☑ Student's folder

For the leader:
☑ Stapler and staples

Session Preparation:

Gather the needed materials.

Session:

- Distribute the students' folders.
- Check to see that each student has completed *Learning Sheet #4*. Then have the students put the activity sheet into their folders. Have the students put their papers in order and staple the edge of each folder so the papers will not fall out.
- Have the students go through their folders. As they look at each sheet, allow the students to share the statements their parents made. Ask the students if this was information they knew before they completed the *Learning Sheets* with their parents. Use every opportunity to emphasize the importance of learning.
- Thank the students for their cooperation and allow them to take their folders home to share with their parents.

BEHAVIOR

Anger (Grades 1-3)

Facing Reality (Grades 1-3)

Attention-Seeking (Grades K-3)

Controlling Anger (Grades 1-3)

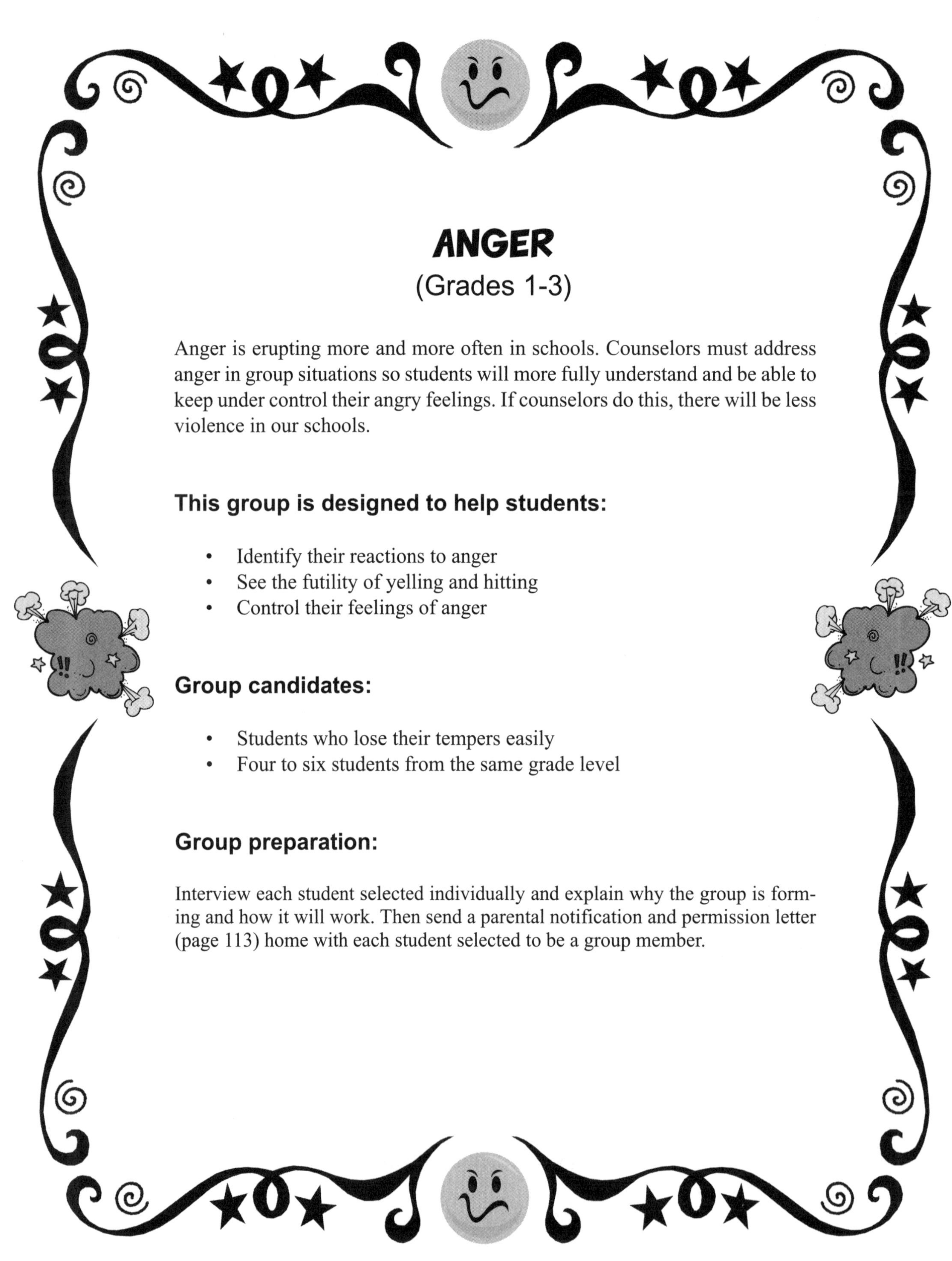

ANGER

(Grades 1-3)

Anger is erupting more and more often in schools. Counselors must address anger in group situations so students will more fully understand and be able to keep under control their angry feelings. If counselors do this, there will be less violence in our schools.

This group is designed to help students:

- Identify their reactions to anger
- See the futility of yelling and hitting
- Control their feelings of anger

Group candidates:

- Students who lose their tempers easily
- Four to six students from the same grade level

Group preparation:

Interview each student selected individually and explain why the group is forming and how it will work. Then send a parental notification and permission letter (page 113) home with each student selected to be a group member.

Dear ____,

Anger is an acceptable emotion, but reactions to anger are not always acceptable. Students usually express their anger in ways that make things worse. Their behaviors may compound the problem or they may get into trouble with an adult.

Students must learn how to control their angry feelings and how to use strategies that will get their angry message across in a positive manner. Your child's classroom teacher has identified your child as a student who could use extra help in this area.

To help your child and others overcome this problem, I am forming a counseling group that will focus on understanding feelings of anger and learning ways to deal appropriately with angry feelings.

Each of the six group meetings will be approximately 30-minutes long. The meetings will be held at a time the classroom teacher selects.

Your child knows about the group and has indicated that he or she would like to participate in it. However, no child is ever included in a small-group counseling program without his or her parents' knowledge and permission.

Please indicate, by completing the form below, that you wish to have your child participate in this group or that you do not want him or her to be included.

Return the permission slip to me by ______________________.

Thank you,

✂- -

☐ I, ______________________________, ***give permission*** for my child to participate in the small-group counseling program on anger control.

☐ I, ______________________________, ***do not give permission*** for my child to participate in the small-group counseling program on anger control.

Child's Name ______________________________ Date ____________

School ______________________________ Grade ____________

Teacher ______________________________

Home Phone (____) ______________ Work Phone (____) ____________

Parent's Printed Name ______________________________

Parent's Signature ______________________________

Session 1: Anger
REACTIONS TO ANGER

Objective:

To introduce students to the topic of anger and have them demonstrate ways they react to certain anger-producing situations

Materials Needed:

For each student:
- ☑ 3 sheets of drawing paper
- ☑ Crayons or markers

For the leader:
- ☑ Chalkboard and chalk or chart paper and marker

Session Preparation:

Gather the necessary materials.

Session:

- Begin the session by doing several things that demonstrate anger (yelling at someone, stamping your feet, hitting a wall, making an angry facial expression, etc.).
- Ask the students why they think you are behaving this way. (I am angry.)
- Discuss the angry actions one at a time. Then ask the students to guess what caused your anger. Write the students' answers on the board/chart paper.
- Distribute three sheets of paper and crayons or markers to each student. Have the students write their names on their papers.
- Give the following directions:

  Use one sheet of paper to draw a picture of what could make you yell at a someone. (Pause until the students have drawn the picture.)

  On another piece of paper, draw a picture of what could make you hit another person. (Pause until the students have drawn the picture.)

  On the last blank piece of paper, draw an angry face. (Pause until the students have drawn the picture.)

- Have the students share their completed pictures with the group.
- Conclude the session by telling the students that everyone feels anger at one time or another. Be sure they realize there is nothing wrong with feeling angry, but that the way people behave when they are angry sometimes needs to be changed.
- Tell the students that the next five sessions will be about what makes them angry, how they behave when they are angry, and ways to react when they are angry without getting into trouble.
- Collect the drawings and save them for subsequent sessions. Gather any the other distributed materials.

Session 2: Anger
YELLING

Objective:

To help students learn appropriate ways of dealing with anger-provoking situations that might cause them to yell at someone

Materials Needed:

For each student:
- ☐ None

For the leader:
- ☑ Chalkboard and chalk or chart paper and marker
- ☑ Students' Session 1 illustrations of situations that could make them yell

Session Preparation:

Gather the necessary materials.

Session:

- Review the students' illustrations of behaviors that could make them angry enough to yell. Then say:

  Yelling is probably the most common reaction to anger. Why do you think this is so? (Yelling is the first reaction most people have when something makes them angry. Yelling may not get someone into trouble or it may get someone into less trouble than other reactions, so a person may have less fear of the consequences.)

- Return each student's drawing. Have the students look at their drawings. Then ask:

  What did the person in the drawing do to make you angry?

  How do you think the angry situation ended?

  Is this something the person does often?

  What other things could this person do to make you want to yell?

- Have each student exchange his/her paper with another group member. Tell the students to look at the papers, pretend they are in the situations illustrated in the drawings, and think of a way to react without yelling. Explain that they shouldn't do anything that would get them into trouble. In other words, they are allowed to feel their anger, but they must control it.

- As the students describe how they could appropriately react to the situations, write their suggestions on the board/chart paper. If not mentioned, add the following suggestions to the list:

  – Walk away from the person.
  – Ignore the person.
  – Calmly tell the person that you do not like the way he/she is behaving.

- Have the students return the papers to their owners. Tell the students to look at the list of reactions on the board/chart paper and select one reaction to use the next time someone yells at them or they feel like yelling at someone.

- Collect the drawings and save them for the next session. Collect any materials that were distributed.

Session 3: Anger
HITTING

Objective:

To help students learn appropriate ways of dealing with anger-provoking situations that might cause them to hit someone

Materials Needed:

For each student:
- ☐ None

For the leader:
- ☑ Chalkboard and chalk or chart paper and marker
- ☑ Students' Session 1 illustrations

Session Preparation:

Gather the necessary materials.

Session:

- Review the students' illustrations of behaviors that could make them angry enough to hit. Then say:

  Hitting is one of the reactions to anger that gets people into trouble. Why do you think people hit other people? (People sometimes hit because they get angry and want to physically lash out at the person who provoked them or because they were hit first and want to strike back.)

  Why is hitting not a good way to handle anger? (You could hurt someone, the force of your blow could cause someone to fall against something and break it, etc.)

- Return each student's drawing of a situation that could make him/her want to hit someone. Have the students look at their drawings and describe the situation that could make them angry enough to hit someone. To help them do this, ask:

  What did the person in the drawing do to make you angry?

  How do you think the angry situation ended?

  Is this something the person does often?

  What other things could this person do to make you want to hit?

- Have the students exchange their papers with someone other than the group member they exchanged papers with in Session 2. Tell the students to look at the papers, pretend they are in the situations illustrated in the drawings, and think of a way to react to the situations without hitting. Explain that they should not do anything that would get them into trouble. Remind them that they are allowed to feel their anger, but they must control it.

- Ask the students to describe what they would do in each situation. Write their suggestions on the board/chart paper.

- Tell the students to look at the list of reactions on the board/chart paper and select one reaction to use the next time they want to hit someone.

- Have the students return the papers to their owners. Remind the students that physical violence is never acceptable.

- Return the other two drawings the student did in Session 1. Tell the students they may take their drawings home.

Session 4: Anger
SAVING FACE

Objective:

To teach students appropriate ways of dealing with anger-provoking situations when friends encourage them to retaliate

Materials Needed:

For each student:
- ☐ None

For the leader:
- ☐ None

Session Preparation:

None required.

Session:

- Tell the students that they are going to talk about ways to control anger when their friends are goading them to retaliate in a way that could get them into trouble.
- Read aloud the following descriptions of two situations:

  Mark and Jerome are playing ball at recess. One boy is playing in one game and the other boy is playing in another. A ball is thrown at Jerome. In order to catch the ball, Jerome has to run into Mark's game. Just at the moment he does this, a ball comes toward Mark. Mark runs to get the ball, but Jerome pushes him out of the way as he catches his ball. Mark's ball goes out into the field and his team loses the game. Mark is so angry that he pushes Jerome to the ground and hits him. Jerome is angry, but he gets up and starts to walk away. Jerome's teammates see what he is doing and yell at him, "C'mon Jerome! Are you going to let him get away with that?"

  Mattie and Lena are washing their hands in the girls' room. Priscilla comes in and bumps into Lena. Lena's purse falls to the floor and all her things fall out of it. Priscilla isn't paying attention and slips on a tube of lip gloss that fell out of Lena's purse. She turns to Lena and punches her in the arm. Lena is getting madder by the minute. First Priscilla bumped into her, then her things were all over the floor, next her lip gloss was smashed, and now she is being punched. She has had it! Priscilla starts to walk away and Mattie says to Lena, "What's the matter with you? Nobody would believe this. Are you going to just let her walk out of here?"

- Discuss the following questions with the students:

  What is the best thing to do when you are angry and know that if you react physically you will get into trouble?

  What is the best thing to do when you are angry and know that if you react physically you probably will get away with it?

  What do you tell your friends when they want you to fight and you do not want to fight?

  What do you tell your friends when they call you names like "chicken" or "wimp" because you do not want to fight?

- Select two pairs of students to role-play the two situations described at the beginning of the session. Explain that they should resolve the situation in a way that wouldn't cause trouble. Emphasize that a student may fall down during the role-play, but that no one may push another person.

- Conclude the session by discussing the suggestions presented in the role-plays.

Session 5: Anger
HOLDING ANGER IN

Objective:

To help students understand the dangers of holding anger in and how to let it out in a positive manner

Materials Needed:

For each student:
- ☐ None

For the leader:
- ☑ Chalkboard and chalk or chart paper and marker

Session Preparation:

Gather the necessary materials.

Session:

- Introduce the lesson by saying:

  In previous sessions, we talked about obvious ways to show anger. Everyone knows a person who yells or hits is angry. In this session, we are going to talk about times when you keep your anger inside yourself and do not show it.

- Ask the students:

  Can you name some reasons you might keep your anger inside?

- Write the students' answers on the board/chart paper. If not mentioned, include the ideas that they may not know how to express their anger toward an authority figure and/or that their anger is embarrassing and they do not want anyone to know about it.

- Read the following examples aloud to the group. Have the students answer the questions following each example:

  Maura is angry because she is not allowed to go on a sleepover with her friends. She does not want to argue with her parents, because she knows they will only get angry at her. If they do, she might be grounded. Maura decides to ignore the fact that she is angry. She believes that if she does, the anger will go away.

  Will the anger go away? (No.)

  What could happen to Maura if she hides her anger? (The anger will stay with her and she will never learn how to talk with her parents about her feelings.)

  Jared refuses to speak to his friends. Last week, they all went to a movie and did not invite him to go. He has decided that if that is the way they want to treat him, he will have nothing more to do with them.

  Can Jared get rid of his anger by avoiding people? (No.)

  What could happen to Jared if he continues to avoid his friends? (His friends may decide he doesn't want to be friends with them and permanently exclude him from their group.)

- Tell the students that in each of the examples they have just heard, the person's actions did not get rid of his/her anger. The only way to get rid of anger would have been to discuss the problem with the people who were causing it.

- Select students to role-play each of the situations you have described. Reread the description of each situation. Have the selected students role-play ways of discussing the situation rather than keeping their anger inside.

- Conclude the session by telling the students that keeping anger inside is like waiting for a time bomb to explode. It would be better to disarm the bomb before it explodes.

Session 6: Anger
CONTROLLING ANGER

Objective:

To help students learn and practice strategies for controlling anger

Materials Needed:

For each student:

☐ None

For the leader:

☑ Copy of *Anger-Control Strategies* (page 122)
☑ Tagboard or cardstock
☑ Scissors
☑ Pillow

Session Preparation:

Reproduce the *Anger-Control Strategies* on tagboard/cardstock. Cut apart the strategies and laminate them for durability (optional). Gather the other necessary materials.

Session:

- Tell the students that they will be learning some ways to control their anger. This does not mean that they will not get angry. It doesn't mean that they will not discuss their anger. It means they will learn some helpful ways to cope with their angry feelings.

- Divide the students into pairs. Give each pair an *Anger-Control Strategy*. (*Note:* If there are cards left over, give some pairs more than one card.) Then give the following directions:

  You are to work together and present the strategy on your card to the rest of the group. Read the strategy written on the card. An additional explanation or an activity for the class to do together is included in parentheses. Do whatever the card says.

- Have each pair of students present its *Anger-Control Strategy* to the rest of the group.

- Conclude the session by asking the students to complete the following sentences aloud:

  In this group, I learned to control my anger by ______.

  I plan to use this strategy when ______.

- Collect any distributed materials.

- Thank the students for participating in the group. Let them know that you are available to meet with them if they feel they cannot control their anger or if they would like to discuss any other issue.

ANGER-CONTROL STRATEGY:
Exercise. *(Have the students stand and jog in place for two minutes. Then say, "Exercising when you get angry will help you control your anger.")*

ANGER-CONTROL STRATEGY:
Concentrate on something else. *(Tell the students they can work a crossword puzzle, a jigsaw puzzle, or anything that will help take their minds off their anger.)*

ANGER-CONTROL STRATEGY:
Punch a pillow, balloon, or bop bag. *(Punch the pillow. Tell the students that this will help them vent their anger without hurting anyone.)*

ANGER-CONTROL STRATEGY:
Breathe deeply. *(Have the students take a deep breath and count to 10. Then have them close their eyes and breathe deeply until they feel the anger leave their bodies.)*

ANGER-CONTROL STRATEGY:
Cry, scream, or yell. *(Tell the students that if they get angry and want to release some emotion, they should find a place where they will not disturb anyone and go ahead and cry, scream, or yell. Have the students name some places where they can do this.)*

ANGER-CONTROL STRATEGY:
Turn on relaxing music. *(Tell the students that listening to relaxing music will take their minds off their anger and calm them down.)*

ANGER-CONTROL STRATEGY:
Try different things to make you calm. *(Have the students suggest things that make them feel calm.)*

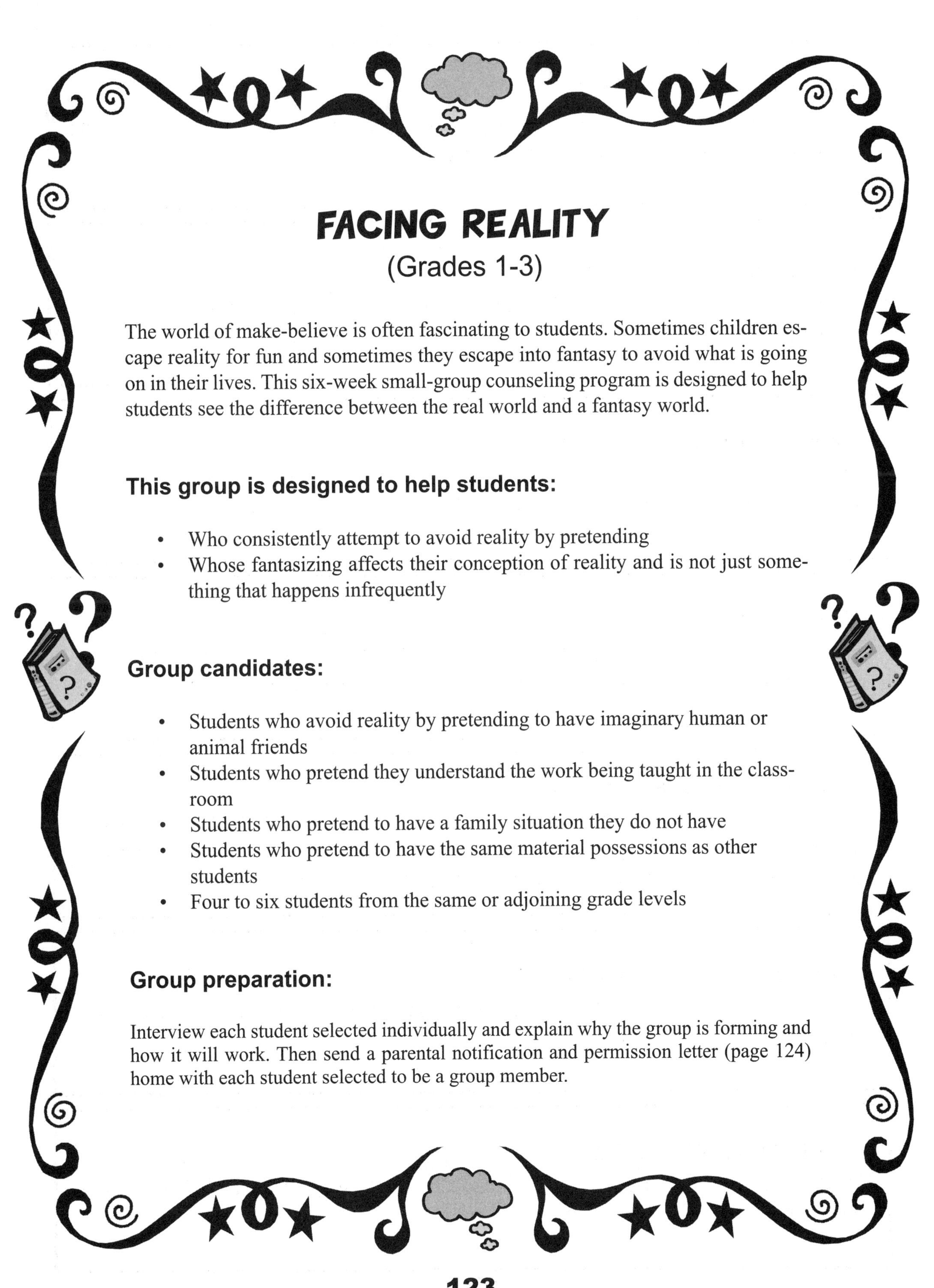

FACING REALITY

(Grades 1-3)

The world of make-believe is often fascinating to students. Sometimes children escape reality for fun and sometimes they escape into fantasy to avoid what is going on in their lives. This six-week small-group counseling program is designed to help students see the difference between the real world and a fantasy world.

This group is designed to help students:

- Who consistently attempt to avoid reality by pretending
- Whose fantasizing affects their conception of reality and is not just something that happens infrequently

Group candidates:

- Students who avoid reality by pretending to have imaginary human or animal friends
- Students who pretend they understand the work being taught in the classroom
- Students who pretend to have a family situation they do not have
- Students who pretend to have the same material possessions as other students
- Four to six students from the same or adjoining grade levels

Group preparation:

Interview each student selected individually and explain why the group is forming and how it will work. Then send a parental notification and permission letter (page 124) home with each student selected to be a group member.

Dear ____:

The world of make-believe is often fascinating for young students. It is a place where they can avoid reality. When this behavior becomes consistent and students use their pretend world to escape from developing friendships, family situations, and academic expectations or pretend to have the same material possessions as other students even though they do not, it is time to address the problem in a way the student will accept.

Students need to learn the difference between *fact* and *fantasy*. Your child's classroom teacher has identified your child as a student who could use extra help in this area.

To help your child and other students overcome this difficulty, I am forming a counseling group that will focus on facing reality and distinguishing fact from fantasy.

Each of the six group meetings will be approximately 30-minutes long. The meetings will be held at a time the classroom teacher selects.

Your child knows about the group and has indicated that he or she would like to participate in it. However, no child is ever included in a small-group counseling program without his or her parents' knowledge and permission.

Please indicate, by completing the form below, that you wish to have your child participate in this group or that you do not want him or her to be included.

Return the permission slip to me by ______________________.

Thank you,

✂- -

☐ I, ________________________________, ***give permission*** for my child to participate in the small-group counseling program on facing reality.

☐ I, ________________________________, ***do not give permission*** for my child to participate in the small-group counseling program on facing reality.

Child's Name ______________________________ Date ____________

School ______________________________ Grade ____________

Teacher ______________________________

Home Phone (____) ____________ Work Phone (____) ____________

Parent's Printed Name ______________________________

Parent's Signature ______________________________

Session 1: Facing Reality
INTRODUCTION: FACT OR FANTASY?

Objective:

To discuss pretending and to experience pretending in selected situations

Materials Needed:

For each student:
- ☐ None

For the leader:
- ☑ Paper
- ☑ Pencil

Session Preparation:

Make a list of places and situations. Places could include being in the mountains, riding in an airplane, floating on a raft in a lake, etc. Situations could include being home with no one to play with, having no bicycle to ride with friends, hearing one's parents are divorcing, etc. Include as many places and situations as you believe you will use in the time allotted for the group session. Gather any other needed materials.

Session:

- Begin the session by having the students define *pretend*. Do this by having group members introduce themselves by completing the following sentence: "My name is _______ and I like to pretend that _______________."
- Have the group discuss the many different reasons students pretend. (*Note:* Be sure that one of the reasons mentioned is *to escape reality.*)
- Ask the students to name the body part that helps them pretend. When the word *brain* is mentioned, have the students explain why this is true. (It is true because pretending is something done in the mind.)
- Introduce the game *Mind Escape*. Explain that you will read a list of places and situations aloud and the students are to pretend they are in these different places or situations.
- Have the students move to places in the room where they feel they can concentrate.
- When the students have settled into their places, tell them that in order to escape into their minds, they must *really* think. Also tell them that when you ask what each place is like, they should say out loud whatever they are thinking.
- Begin by reciting the selected places one at a time. After mentioning each place, allow time for the students to concentrate on it and pretend they are actually there. Then ask the students to describe the place.
- Present the situations one at a time. After each situation is presented, give the students time to imagine they are actually in that situation. Then ask the students how being in the situation makes them feel.
- Conclude the session by telling the students they have just spent time pretending to be in different places and situations. Ask them to remember all the times they pretend between now and the next group session.

Session 2: Facing Reality
STORY STARTER

Objective:

To have the students first create stories about people who pretend in order to escape real life, then create stories in which they face reality

Materials Needed:

For each student (if the students are writing a story of their own at each session):

☑ Composition book
☑ Pencil

For the leader:

☑ Chalkboard and chalk or chart paper and marker

Session Preparation:

Decide whether the story will be completed by the group as a whole or by each individual student. Gather the necessary materials.

Session:

- If the students are writing stories of their own distribute a composition book and pencil to each child.
- Write the *Story Starter* and list of helping words on the board/chart paper.
- Rcad aloud the following *Story Starter* and list of helping words to the students:

  Everyone but Mary was outside playing. She had been asked to play, but she told her friends that she wasn't allowed outside. She told herself it didn't matter because she would have just as much fun playing in her room.

  Helping Words:

  looked
  lonely
  play
  talk
  laugh

- If the students are writing stories of their own, tell them to write an ending to the story about Mary. The story should use each helping word at least once.
- If the students are not writing stories of their own, have the students verbally relate an ending to the story. The story should use each helping word at least once.
- Then discuss the following questions:

  What caused Mary to act the way she did?

  How did Mary avoid facing reality?

- Using the same *Story Starter,* conclude the session by writing a group story on the board/chart paper. In this version of the story, have the students verbally describe how Mary could face reality.

Session 3: Facing Reality
STORY STARTER

Objective:

To have the students create stories about people who pretend in order to escape real life

Materials Needed:

For each student (if the students are writing a story of their own at each session):

☑ Composition book
☑ Pencil

For the leader (if the stories for each session are to be completed as a group):

☑ Chalkboard and chalk or chart paper and marker

Session Preparation:

Decide whether the story will be completed by the group as a whole or by each individual student. Gather the necessary materials.

Session:

- If the students are writing stories of their own distribute a composition book and pencil to each child.

- Write the *Story Starter* and list of helping words on the board/chart paper.

- Read aloud the following *Story Starter* and list of helping words to the students:

  Mike's papers always had a lot of mistakes. When the teacher or his parents asked Mike if he needed help , he always said, "No."

  Helping Words:

  boring
  understand
  care
  work
  smart

- If the students are writing stories of their own, tell them to write an ending to the story about Mike. The story should use each helping word at least once.

- If the students are not writing stories of their own, have the students verbally relate an ending to the story. The story should use each helping word at least once.

- Then discuss the following questions:

  What caused Mike to act the way he did?

  How did Mike avoid facing reality?

- Using the same *Story Starter,* conclude the session by writing a group story on the board/chart paper. In this version of the story, have the students verbally describe how Mike could face reality.

Session 4: Facing Reality
STORY STARTER

Objective:

To have the students create stories about people who pretend in order to escape real life

Materials Needed:

For each student (if the students are writing a story of their own at each session):

☑ Composition book
☑ Pencil

For the leader (if the stories for each session are to be completed as a group):

☑ Chalkboard and chalk or chart paper and marker

Session Preparation:

Decide whether the story will be completed by the group as a whole or by each individual student. Gather the necessary materials.

Session:

- If the students are writing stories of their own distribute a composition book and pencil to each child.
- Write the *Story Starter* and list of helping words on the board/chart paper.
- Read aloud thc following *Story Starter* and list of helping words to the students:

  The bike trip was set for Saturday morning, and all of Cindy's friends were going. Cindy didn't want her friends to know her mother couldn't afford to buy her a bike.

  Helping Words:

  busy
  hate
  fun
  rain
  dangerous

- If the students are writing stories of their own, tell them to write an ending to the story about Cindy. The story should use each helping word at least once.
- If the students are not writing stories of their own, have the students verbally relate an ending to the story. The story should use each helping word at least once.
- Then discuss the following questions:

  What caused Cindy to act the way she did?

  How did Cindy avoid facing reality?

- Using the same *Story Starter,* conclude the session by writing a group story on the board/chart paper. In this version of the story, have the students verbally describe how Cindy could face reality.

Session 5: Facing Reality
STORY STARTER

Objective:

To have the students create stories about people who pretend in order to escape real life

Materials Needed:

For each student (if the students are writing a story of their own at each session):

- ☑ Composition book
- ☑ Pencil

For the leader (if the stories for each session are to be completed as a group):

- ☑ Chalkboard and chalk or chart paper and marker

Session Preparation:

Decide whether the story will be completed by the group as a whole or by each individual student. Gather the necessary materials.

Session:

- If the students are writing stories of their own distribute a composition book and pencil to each child.
- Write the *Story Starter* and list of helping words on the board/chart paper.
- Read aloud the following *Story Starter* and list of helping words to the students:

  Juan's father had moved out of the house. He had said he would see Juan soon, but that was two weeks ago. Juan really wanted his father to move back home. He didn't want his friends to know that he was upset about his parents' situation.

  Helping Words:

  trip
  telephone
  present
  wants
  often

- If the students are writing stories of their own, tell them to write an ending to the story about Juan. The story should use each helping word at least once.
- If the students are not writing stories of their own, have the students verbally relate an ending to the story. The story should use each helping word at least once.
- Then discuss the following questions:

  What caused Juan to act the way he did?

  How did Juan avoid facing reality?

- Using the same *Story Starter,* conclude the session by writing a group story on the board/chart paper. In this version of the story, have the students verbally describe how Juan could face reality.

Session 6: Facing Reality
FANTASY VERSUS REALITY

Objective:

To discuss why students do not want to face reality and why they must eventually face reality

Materials Needed:

For each student:
- ☐ None

For the leader:
- ☐ None

Session Preparation:

None required

Session:

- Satisfy the purpose of the session by having a group discussion on the following questions:

  Why do some students not want to face reality? (Be sure the students' answers include the fact that real situations are sometimes painful.)

  What do students think will happen if they pretend painful or unpleasant situations do not exist? (They think that if they avoid the situation, their hurt feelings will go away.)

  Does reality go away? (No.)

  What happens if a student never accepts reality? (The student lives in a pretend world and does not learn to live in a real world. The student does not learn to face situations, only to escape from them.)

  Why is it better to live in a real world? (A who student hides from situations in the real world does not learn to understand situations, to cope with problems, or to relate honestly to other people.)

- Conclude the last session by asking each group member to tell a story about him/herself and include what he/she does to avoid a situation which he/she does not like. Each group member should conclude their story by describing what he/she must do in order to face reality.

ATTENTION-SEEKING

(Grades K-3)

Many young students seek attention. They do this in order to feel a sense of belonging and acceptance that positive behaviors do not give them and because they mistakenly believe that behaving in a negative manner assures them of at least some recognition. This behavior annoys and irritates others, whose responses give these students the false sense that they are being accepted.

This group is designed to help students:

- Realize that everyone needs attention
- Identify ways that others get attention
- Learn the differences between positive and negative ways to get attention
- Identify ways each student gets attention
- Choose positive ways to get attention in the future

Group candidates:

- Students who demand attention from everyone around them
- Students who constantly call out, interrupt, drop things, make noises, get out of their seats, and annoy others.
- Four to six students from the same or adjoining grade levels

Group preparation:

Interview each student selected individually and explain why the group is forming and how it will work. Then send a parental notification and permission letter (page 132) home with each student selected to be a group member.

Dear ____,

It is very common for young students to seek attention. This behavior can be positive or negative. When students interrupt, talk out of turn, drop things, make noises, get out of their seats at inappropriate times, etc., their negative attention-seeking behaviors annoy others.

Students need to learn how to identify their negative attention-seeking behaviors and choose positive ways to interact with others. Your child's classroom teacher has identified your child as a student who could use extra help in this area.

To help your child and others overcome this difficulty, I am forming a counseling group that will focus on helping students understand their attention-seeking misbehaviors and learn ways to change them into positive attention-seeking behaviors.

Each of the six group meetings will be approximately 30-minutes long. The meetings will be held at a time the classroom teacher selects.

Your child knows about the group and has indicated that he or she would like to participate in it. However, no child is ever included in a small-group counseling program without his or her parents' knowledge and permission.

Please indicate, by completing the form below, that you wish to have your child participate in this group or that you do not want him or her to be included.

Return the permission slip to me by ______________________.

Thank you,

✂- -

☐ I, __________________________________, ***give permission*** for my child to participate in the small-group counseling program on attention-seeking behaviors.

☐ I, __________________________________, ***do not give permission*** for my child to participate in the small-group counseling program on attention-seeking behaviors.

Child's Name ______________________________ Date ____________

School ____________________________________ Grade ____________

Teacher ___________________________________

Home Phone (____) _____________ Work Phone (____) _____________

Parent's Printed Name _________________________

Parent's Signature ___________________________

Session 1: Attention-Seeking

WHAT IS ATTENTION-SEEKING?

Objective:

To introduce students to the topic of attention-seeking and help them realize that everyone needs attention

Materials Needed:

For each student:

☑ Copy of *This Person Needs Attention Because ...*(page 135)
☑ Crayons or markers
☑ Pencil

For the leader:

☑ Folder to store students' papers

Session Preparation:

Reproduce *This Person Needs Attention Because ...* for each student. Gather the other necessary materials.

Session:

- Begin the group by presenting the following rules to the students. (*Note:* This is especially important for a group dedicated to this topic.)

  1. You must listen when someone else is speaking.
  2. Everyone will have a turn to talk.
  3. Put-downs or other negative statements about anyone in the group are not allowed.

- Ask each student to state his/her name and one thing he/she likes to eat.

- Introduce the topic of attention-seeking by asking:

  What do you think attention-seeking *means?* (Doing something in order to be noticed by others.)

  How do people get attention? (People get attention by doing something others notice like winning a contest, getting into trouble, being famous, etc.)

  How does your teacher get attention? (Accept all appropriate answers.)

  How do your parents get attention? (Accept all appropriate answers.)

  How do you get attention? (Accept all appropriate answers.)

  Why do people need attention? (We feel good when we are noticed. Accept any other appropriate answers.)

- Distribute *This Person Needs Attention Because ...*, a pencil, and crayons or markers to each student. Have the students write their name and grade on the activity sheet. Then tell them to draw a picture of a person. They may draw an entire person or just a head. The students should then think about how that person feels and draw a face to express that feeling.

- On the line at the bottom of the page, complete the sentence telling why the person needs attention. (Sample answers could be because she is sad, because he has no one to play with, etc.)

- If there is enough time left in the session, have the students share their drawings with the group.
- Collect the drawings, place them in the folder, and save them for the last session.
- Conclude the session by telling the students to notice how their teachers and parents get attention. They should be ready to share their observations at the next session.

Name ______________________________________ Grade __________

THIS PERSON NEEDS ATTENTION BECAUSE ...

____

Session 2: Attention-Seeking
WAYS ADULTS SEEK ATTENTION

Objective:

To discuss the positive and negative ways teachers and parents seek attention

Materials Needed:

For each student:

☑ Copy of *Five Ways Other People Seek Attention Are ...* (page 137)
☑ Crayons or markers
☑ Pencil

For the leader:

☑ Folder to store students' papers

Session Preparation:

Reproduce *Five Ways Other People Seek Attention Are ...* for each student. Gather the other necessary materials.

Session:

- Review the group rules by asking the students to recall what they learned in Session 1. (*Note:* This is especially important for a group dedicated to this topic,)
- Tell the students what your favorite time of day is, then have each student name his/her favorite time of day.
- Give each student a turn to act out one way he/she saw a teacher or parent seeking attention. Remind the students that their observation may be of a positive or a negative attention-seeking behavior.
- Begin by asking for a volunteer to role-play the attention-seeking behavior he/she observed. The other students should observe the role-play, then guess the behavior. The first student who guesses correctly will be the next actor. Remind them not to mention any names. (*Note:* If the students are in first or early second grade, have each actor whisper into your ear what he/she plans to act out. Then if the group has difficulty guessing the behavior, you may give them verbal clues.)
- Distribute *Five Ways Other People Seek Attention Are ...*, a pencil, and crayons or markers to each student. Have the students write their name and grade on the activity sheet, then draw or write five ways other people get attention.
- Have the students share their completed activity sheets.
- Collect the activity sheets and place them in the folder.
- Conclude the session by telling the students to observe other group members on the playground, in the classroom, in the cafeteria, or on the bus to see what they do to get attention. They should be ready to share their observations at the next session.

Name ____ Grade ___________

FIVE WAYS OTHER PEOPLE SEEK ATTENTION ARE...

Draw a picture of something you saw an adult doing to get attention. He or she may have done a good thing or something that was not so good.

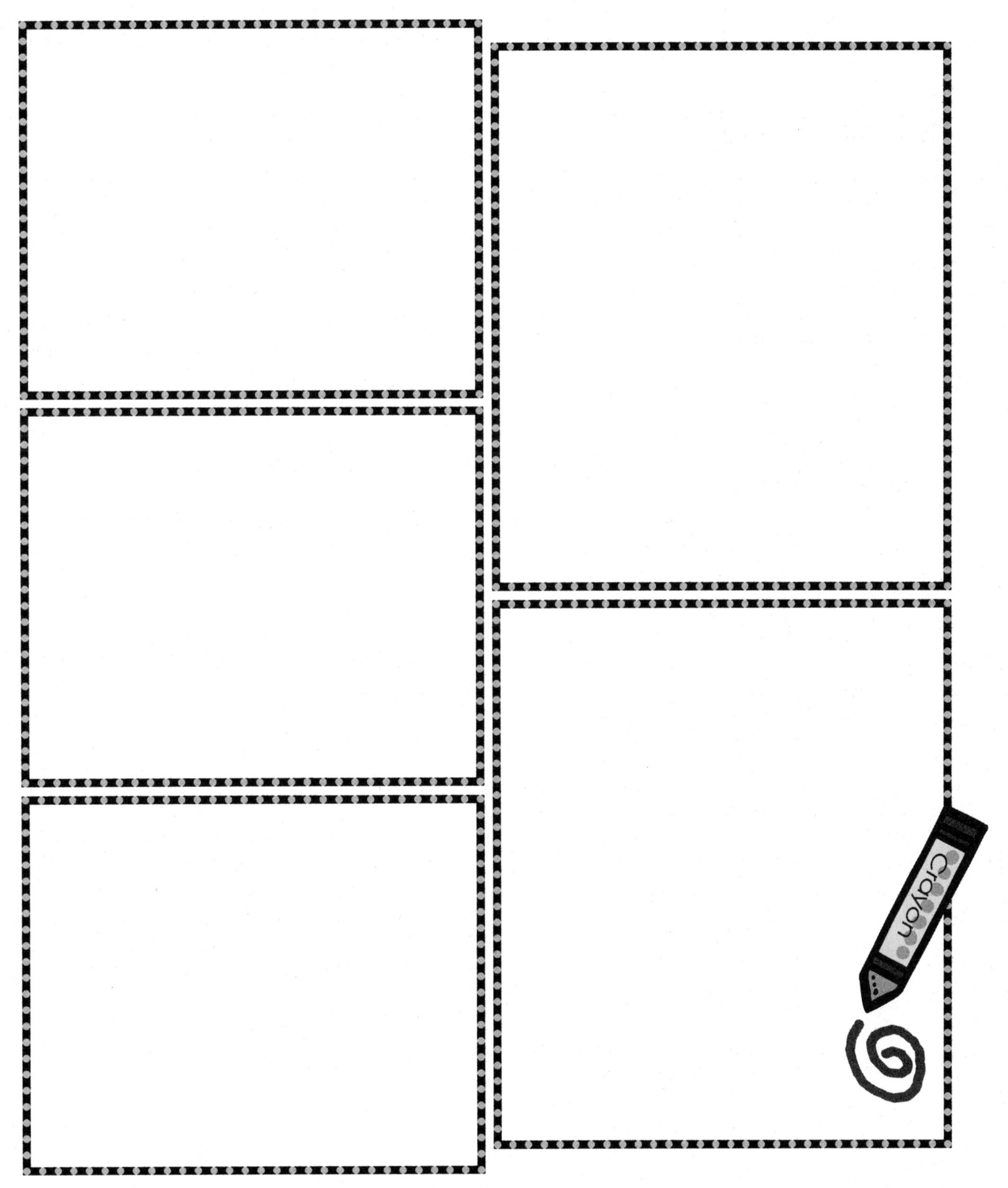

Session 3: Attention-Seeking
PEOPLE FROM WHOM I LIKE TO GET ATTENTION

Objective:

To identify ways students seek attention and identify people from whom students enjoy getting attention

Materials Needed:

For each student:
- ☑ Copy of *Five People From Whom I Like To Get Attention* (page 139)
- ☑ Crayons or markers
- ☑ Pencil

For the leader:
- ☑ Folder to store students' papers

Session Preparation:

Reproduce *Five People From Whom I Like To Get Attention* for each student. Gather the other necessary materials.

Session:

- Review the group rules by asking the students to recall what they learned in Session 1.
- Discuss ways other students seek attention. Then have the students share their observations of ways they have seen group members seeking attention. Remind them not to mention any names.
- Have the students respond to these statements:

  Something someone did to get my attention was ______.

  Something someone did to get my attention that made me angry was ______.

- Distribute *Five People From Whom I Like To Get Attention,* a pencil, and crayons or markers to each student. Have the students write their name and grade on the activity sheet, then write or draw pictures of five people from whom they like to get attention.
- Have the students share their completed activity sheets with the group.
- Collect the activity sheets and place them in the folder.
- Conclude the session by telling the students to pay attention to their own behavior and remember what attention-seeking behaviors they use. Tell the students to be prepared to share their observations at the next session.

Name ______________________________ Grade __________

FIVE PEOPLE FROM WHOM I LIKE TO GET ATTENTION

Draw pictures of and write the names of five people from whom you like to get attention. Draw each person's picture and write his/her name on the line in the frame.

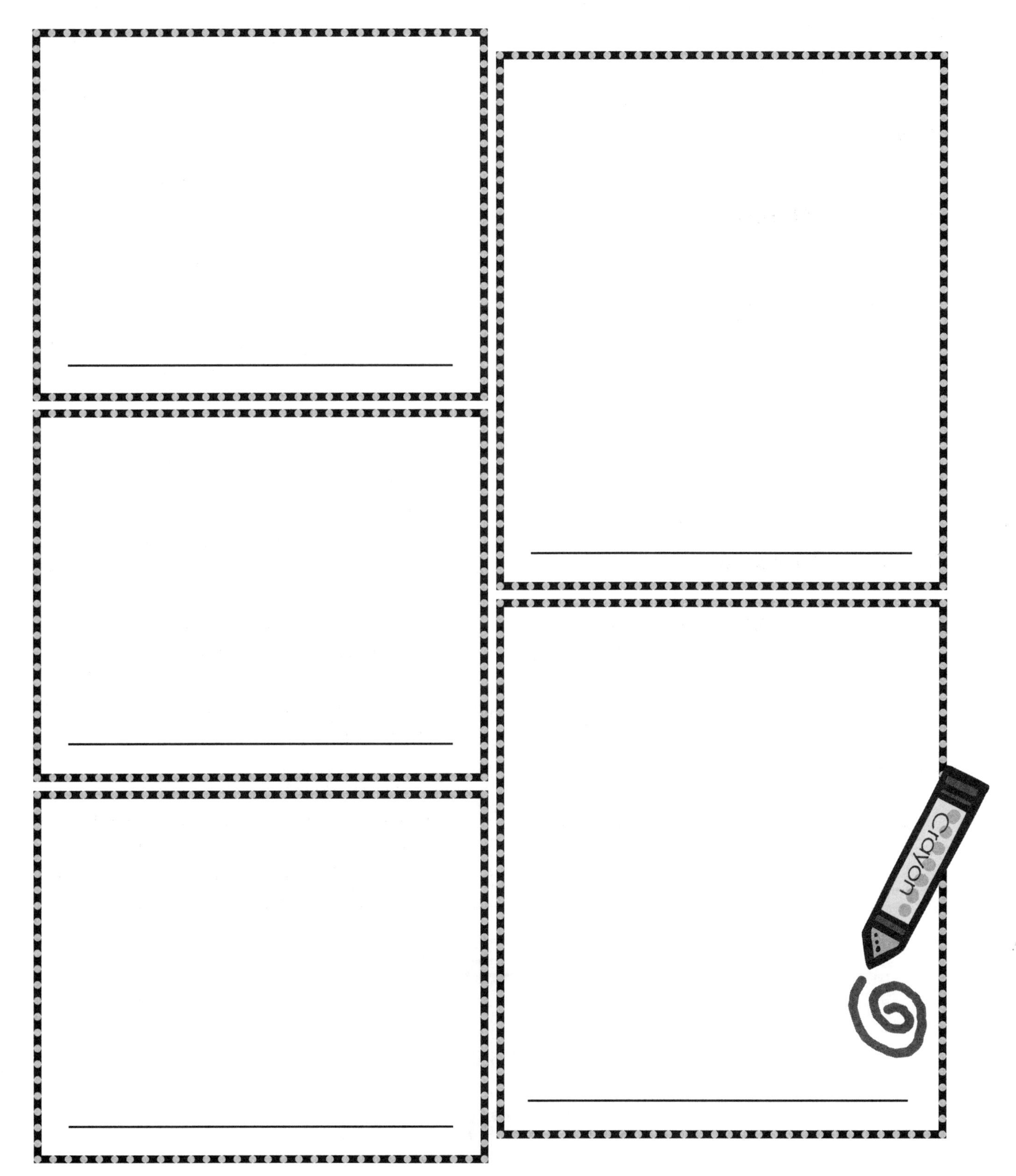

Session 4: Attention-Seeking
WAYS I GET ATTENTION

Objective:

To help students recognize all types of attention-seeking behavior and become aware of the attention-seeking behaviors they use regularly

Materials Needed:

For each student:

- ☑ Copy of *Five Ways I Use To Get Attention Are ...* (page 141)
- ☑ Crayons or markers
- ☑ Pencil

For the leader:

- ☑ Folder to store students' papers
- ☑ Chart paper and marker

Session Preparation:

Reproduce *Five Ways I Use To Get Attention Are ...* for each student. Gather the other necessary materials.

Session:

- Review the group rules by asking the students to recall what they learned in Session 1.
- Have the students share one or more things they have done since the last session to get attention. Tell them to explain why they behaved that way and how they felt about it. Record their contributions on the chart paper. Save the list for the next session.
- Distribute *Five Ways I Use To Get Attention Are ...*, a pencil, and crayons to each student. Have the students write their name and grade on their activity sheet, then draw pictures of five ways they use to get attention.
- Conclude the session by having the students share their activity sheets.
- Collect the activity sheets and place them in the folder.

Name ____ Grade __________

FIVE WAYS I USE TO GET ATTENTION ARE ...

Draw pictures of five ways you use to get attention.

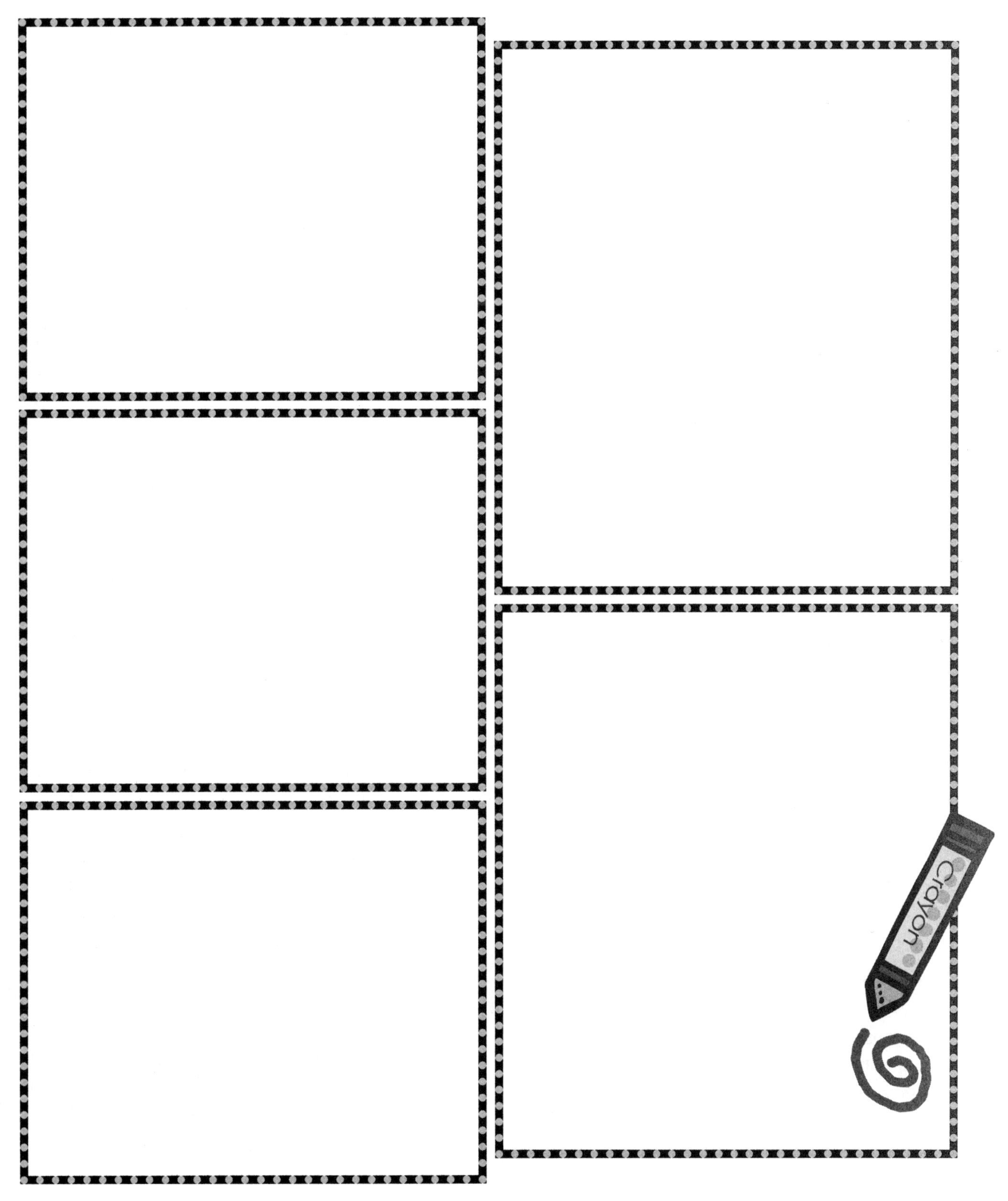

Session 5: Attention-Seeking

POSITIVE VERSUS NEGATIVE ATTENTION-SEEKING BEHAVIORS

Objective:

To help students recognize the differences between positive and negative attention-seeking behaviors

Materials Needed:

For each student:

- ☑ Copy of *Reaching My Goal* (page 144)
- ☑ Crayons or markers
- ☑ Pencil

For the leader:

- ☑ Folder to store students' papers
- ☑ Chart paper and marker
- ☑ List from Session 4
- ☑ Tape

Session Preparation:

Reproduce *Reaching My Goal* for each student. Make two charts on the chart paper. Label one *Positive Ways To Get Attention* and label the other *Negative Ways To Get Attention.* Hang the charts and the list from Session 4 in a place where all the students can see them. Gather the other necessary materials.

Session:

- Discuss positive and negative attention-seeking behaviors. Make sure the students understand the difference between the two. (Positive attention-seeking behavior is when recognition is received for doing something good like completing homework on time, helping a friend, etc. Negative attention-seeking behavior is when recognition is received for doing something disruptive, for breaking rules, or for other misbehaviors.)
- Review the list from the previous session with the students and add any new ideas they may have.
- Point to the charts on positive and negativc attention-seeking behavior. Using the ideas written on the list from Session 4, have the students decide whether each behavior should be listed on the *Positive Ways To Get Attention* chart or on the *Negative Ways To Get Attention* chart. Record the students' decisions on the chart they indicate.
- Using the *Negative Ways To Get Attention* chart, discuss ways negative behaviors can be changed to positive behaviors. Save the charts.
- Tell the students to think of different attention-seeking behaviors. Draw an imaginary line on the floor. Tell the students that each end of the line stands for a different extreme of behavior, such as always interrupting or never interrupting. Label one end *Always-Interrupting Anna* and the other *Never-Interrupting Nick.* Do not use the name of any group member.
- Have the students think about their own behavior, decide where they would be on the line, and move to that spot. Then ask the students to move to the spot where they would like to be.

- Have the students suggest other negative attention-seeking behaviors and their opposites. To add interest, use such names as: Pushes-In-Line Polly and Stands-In-Line Sam or Wandering Willie and Stays-In-Seat Sandra. (*Note:* Do not use any the name of any group member.)

- Distribute *Reaching My Goal*, a pencil, and crayons or markers to each student. Have the students write their name and grade on the activity sheet. Review the activity directions, then have each student draw a football, indicating where he/she is on the field. Then have each student draw a picture of him/herself on the line where he/she would like to be. Have the students decorate their activity sheets.

- Discuss how the students can help the football reach the goal line which, in turn, will put them where they would like to be.

- Collect the activity sheets and place them in the folder.

Name ______________________________ Grade __________

REACHING MY GOAL

Draw a football by the field line that shows how you currently behave. Then draw a picture of yourself by the field line that shows how you would like to behave.

BEHAVE ALL OF THE TIME

BEHAVE MOST OF THE TIME

BEHAVE SOME OF THE TIME

MISBEHAVE SOME OF THE TIME

MISBEHAVE MOST OF THE TIME

MISBEHAVE ALL OF THE TIME

Session 6: Attention-Seeking

SETTING GOALS FOR POSITIVE BEHAVIORS

Objective:

To have the students make a commitment to change negative attention-seeking behavior to positive attention-seeking behavior

Materials Needed:

For each student:

- ☑ Copy of *Ways I Plan To Get Positive Attention* (page 146)
- ☑ Crayons or markers
- ☑ Pencil
- ☑ Piece of construction paper

For the leader:

- ☑ Folder with students' papers
- ☑ *Positive Ways To Get Attention* chart from Session 5
- ☑ Tape

Session Preparation:

Reproduce *Ways I Plan To Get Positive Attention* for each student. Tape the *Positive Ways To Get Attention* chart to the wall or board where all the students can see it. Gather the other necessary materials.

Session:

- Review the *Positive Ways to Get Attention* chart, discussing each item.
- Distribute *Ways I Plan To Get Positive Attention*, a pencil, and crayons or markers to each student. Have the students write their name and grade on the activity sheet, then complete the activity sheet.
- Have the students share their completed activity sheet with the group.
- Tell the students that if they really plan to use what they have drawn or written on their activity sheet, they should sign their name on the line at the bottom of the page. Explain that this is like a contract and that when they sign it, they are agreeing to behave that way.
- Distribute a piece of construction paper to each student. Have the students fold the paper in half, title the front *Good Ways To Seek Attention,* and decorate it any way they choose.
- Distribute the papers collected from the students throughout the group experience. Tell the students to put the activity sheets into their construction paper folders.
- Tell the students that this is their last session and that they may take their folders home with them.
- Conclude the group by thanking the students for their participation. Have each student complete the statement:

  In this group, I learned ______.

Name ______________________________________ Grade ___________

WAYS I PLAN TO GET POSITIVE ATTENTION

Think of five ways you will behave in order to get attention in a positive way. Draw a picture or write a description in each of the five blocks below. When you have finished, sign your name on the line at the bottom of the page if you really plan to behave the way you have said you will.

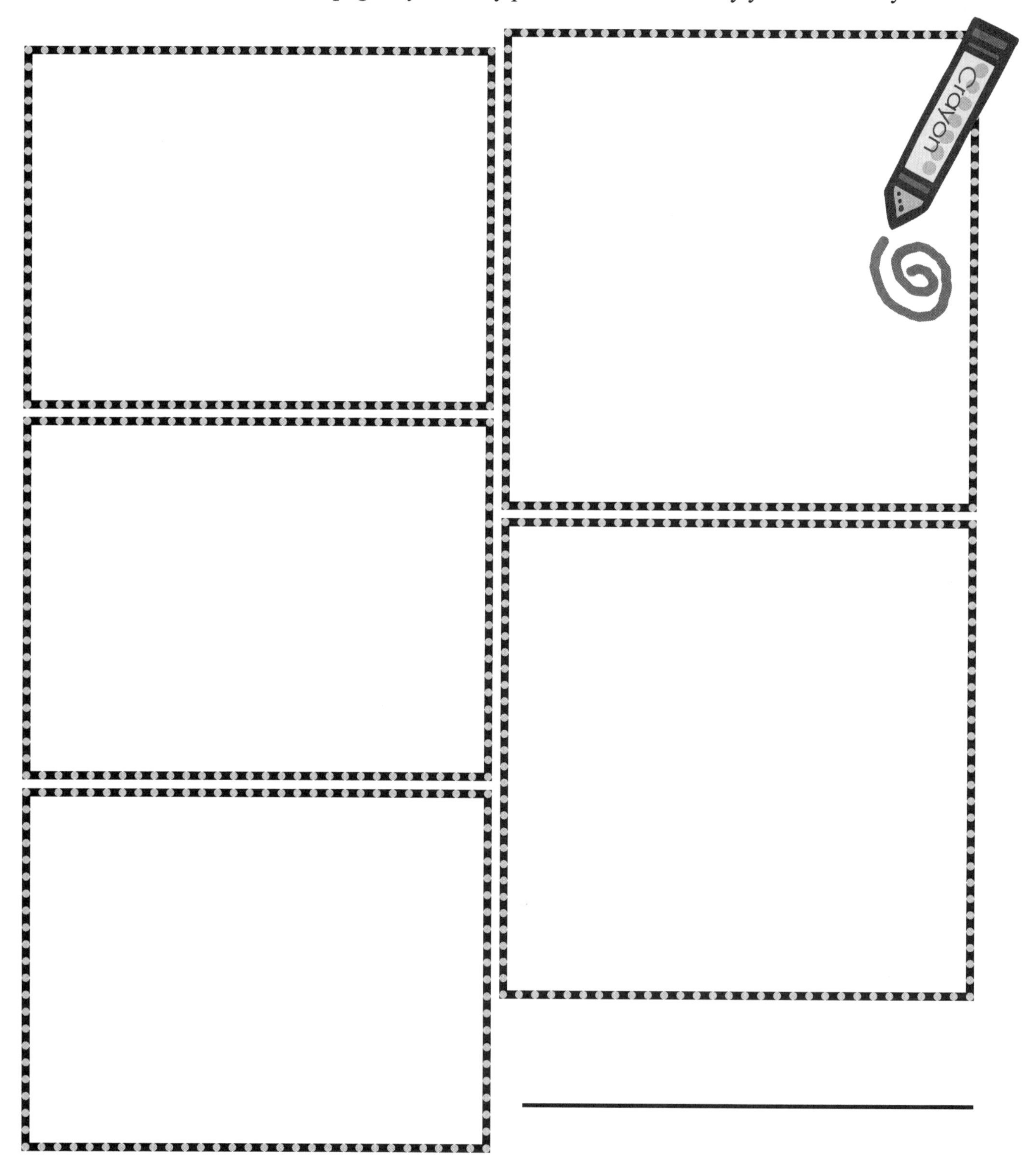

____

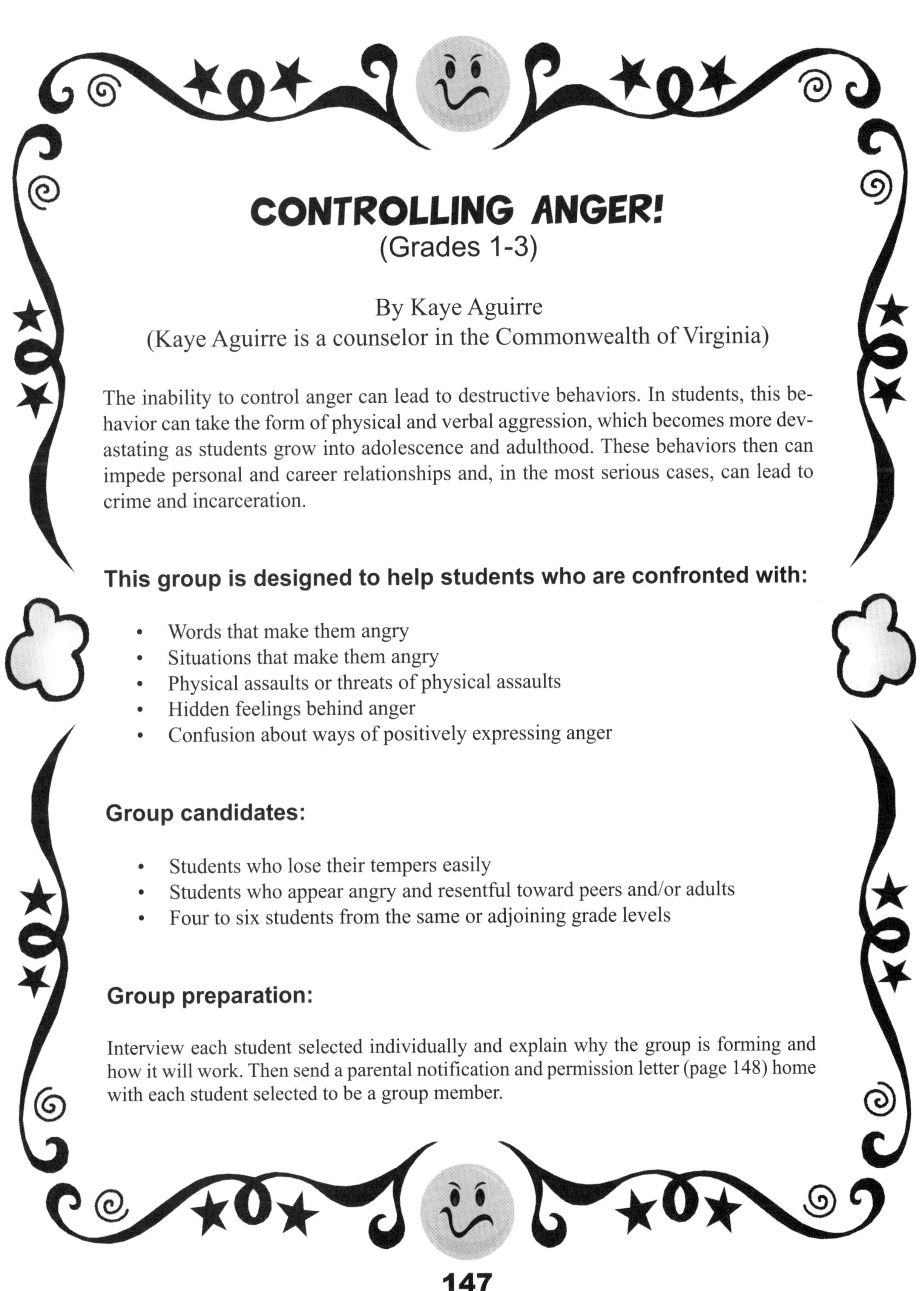

CONTROLLING ANGER!
(Grades 1-3)

By Kaye Aguirre
(Kaye Aguirre is a counselor in the Commonwealth of Virginia)

The inability to control anger can lead to destructive behaviors. In students, this behavior can take the form of physical and verbal aggression, which becomes more devastating as students grow into adolescence and adulthood. These behaviors then can impede personal and career relationships and, in the most serious cases, can lead to crime and incarceration.

This group is designed to help students who are confronted with:

- Words that make them angry
- Situations that make them angry
- Physical assaults or threats of physical assaults
- Hidden feelings behind anger
- Confusion about ways of positively expressing anger

Group candidates:

- Students who lose their tempers easily
- Students who appear angry and resentful toward peers and/or adults
- Four to six students from the same or adjoining grade levels

Group preparation:

Interview each student selected individually and explain why the group is forming and how it will work. Then send a parental notification and permission letter (page 148) home with each student selected to be a group member.

Dear ____:

As part of the guidance program, it is my privilege to provide opportunities for students to meet in small groups. The purpose of these groups is to allow the students acquire information and skills that will help them be more successful in the school setting. School success depends not only on academic ability, but also on relating to others in a positive manner.

Your child has the opportunity to participate in a group called *Controlling Anger*. This group is designed to help students learn how to react when words, situations, physical assaults, or threats make them feel angry.

Each of the seven group meetings will be approximately 30-minutes long. The meetings will be held at a time the classroom teacher selects.

Your child knows about the group and has indicated that he or she would like to participate in it. However, no child is ever included in a small-group counseling program without his or her parents' knowledge and permission.

Please indicate, by completing the form below, that you wish to have your child participate in this group or that you do not want him or her to be included.

Return the permission slip to me by ________________________.

Thank you,

✂- -

☐ I, ____________________________________, ***give permission*** for my child to participate in the small-group counseling program on controlling anger.

☐ I, ____________________________________, ***do not give permission*** for my child to participate in the small-group counseling program on controlling anger.

Child's Name ________________________________ Date ______________

School ______________________________________ Grade ______________

Teacher _____________________________________

Home Phone (_____) ______________ Work Phone (_____) ______________

Parent's Printed Name ___________________________

Parent's Signature ______________________________

Session 1: Controlling Anger!
INTRODUCTION

Objective:

To introduce the students to each other and help them learn the goals and rules of the group

Materials Needed:

For each student:

- ☑ Name tag
- ☑ Pencil
- ☑ Crayons or marker
- ☑ Copy of *Controlling Anger Folder Cover* (page 150)
- ☑ Copy of *Controlling Anger Goals* (page 151)
- ☑ Copy of *Controlling Anger Rules* (page 152)
- ☑ Copy of *Anger Wheel* (page 153)
- ☑ Piece of construction paper
- ☑ Drawing paper
- ☑ Scissors
- ☑ Gluestick

For the leader:

- ☑ Mural paper
- ☑ Tape
- ☑ Stickers

Session Preparation:

Reproduce the *Controlling Anger Folder Cover, Controlling Anger Goals, Controlling Anger Rules,* and *Anger Wheel* for each student. Gather the other materials.

Session:

- Introduce yourself to the group. Then have the groups members introduce themselves.
- Distribute a name tag, a pencil, and crayons or markers to each student. Tell the students to write their names on the tags, then decorate them.
- Distribute the *Controlling Anger Folder Cover, Controlling Anger Goals, Controlling Anger Rules, Anger Wheel,* construction paper, drawing paper, scissors, and a gluestick to each student.
- Have the students fold the construction paper in half and glue the *Folder Cover* to the construction paper.
- Tell the students to look at the seven boxes on the *Controlling Anger Folder Cover*. The boxes are for stickers. At each session, each student will receive a sticker to put in a box. When the boxes are filled, the sessions will be over. Distribute a sticker for each student to put it in the first box.
- Discuss the *Controlling Anger Goals.*
- Review the *Controlling Anger Rules*. Have each student sign the rules if he/she agrees to follow them and is interested in remaining in the group.
- On drawing paper, have each student draw a picture of him/herself, then cut out the picture. Glue the pictures to a large piece of mural paper titled *Anger Managers*. Tape the mural to the wall.
- Instruct the students to write, on the *Anger Wheel* spokes, different things that make them feel angry. Have those students who wish to do so share their completed *Anger Wheels* with the group.
- Have the students place all their papers in their construction paper folders. Collect the folders and any other distributed materials.

CONTROLLING
ANGER!
NAME

GOALS

In this group, I will learn to:

~1~
Handle anger caused by words.

~2~
Handle anger caused by situations.

~3~
Handle anger caused by threats of physical harm.

~4~
Discover feelings hidden behind my anger.

~5~
Handle anger in a helpful way.

~6~
Celebrate my positive choices.

RULES

In this group, I will:

~1~
Respect the privacy of others (confidentiality).

~2~
Not tease others or put them down.

~3~
Listen to others when they speak.

~4~
Keep my hands to myself.

~5~
Be responsible for classwork missed because of group meetings.

SIGNATURE _______________ DATE _______________

Name ____ Grade ___________

Session 2: Controlling Anger!
WORDS CAN MAKE YOU ANGRY

Objective:

To help students learn to handle anger caused by words spoken to them

Materials Needed:

For each student:

- ☑ Copy of *Feelings Wheel* (page 156)
- ☑ Copy of *Activity Sheet #1* (page 158)
- ☑ Copy of *Fact Sheet #1* (page 159)
- ☑ Scissors
- ☑ Brad

For the leader:

- ☑ Students' folders
- ☑ Stickers
- ☑ Square box (like one for a mug)
- ☑ White contact paper or white paint
- ☑ Marker
- ☑ Cardstock or heavyweight paper
- ☑ Copy of *The Smart Fish* (page 157)

Session Preparation:

Reproduce a *Feelings Wheel* on cardstock or heavyweight paper for each student. Reproduce *Activity Sheet #1* and *Fact Sheet #1* for each student. Make a *Feeling Die*. Cover the box with contact paper or white paint. On each side of the box, write an emotion. Use words appropriate for the age level of the students in the group. Reproduce *The Smart Fish* for the leader. Gather the other materials.

Session:

- Distribute the students' folders. Give each student a sticker to place on the cover of his/her folder.
- Tell the students that anger is only one feeling people are capable of expressing. And even though this group deals mainly with controlling and directing anger in a positive manner, it is important to recognize all the feelings we experience.
- Have each member of the group roll the *Feeling Die* and describe a time that a person could feel the emotion it shows.
- Distribute a *Feelings Wheel* for each student to assemble. Have each student turn his/her wheel to show how he/she is feeling. Have those students who wish to do so share how they are feeling with the group.
- Review the goals of the group.
- Tell the students that today they will learn to handle anger caused by words that are spoken to them.
- Read *The Smart Fish* to the students.
- Discuss how to avoid the *bait* of words other people say.
- Distribute *Activity Sheet #1* to each student. Explain that these four pictures can help the students remember how to handle anger caused by spoken words. The first picture represents the *Smart Fish* and its refusal to be *caught* by the *bait* of words.

- Discuss the drawing of the *wall*. Explain that if we don't react to the words someone else is saying, the person will usually choose someone else to pick on. A person gets tired of pushing against wall that will not move!

- Discuss the drawing of a *tennis game*. Explain that no one can make us get involved in his/her game. If we choose not to play, the other person cannot win. We do not have to get involved in other people's games.

- Discuss the drawing of *armor*. Explain that the good feelings we have about ourselves can help protect us from mean things others say. The truth will protect us from the annoying *arrows* (mean words) people say.

- Distribute a copy of *Fact Sheet #1* to each student. Read the sentence and discuss it with the group.

- Have the students place their papers in their folders.

- Collect the folders and any materials that were distributed.

FEELINGS WHEEL

Directions:

1. Cut out the *Feelings Wheel* and the spinner.
2. Use the brad to make a hole. Attach the spinner to the wheel with the brad.

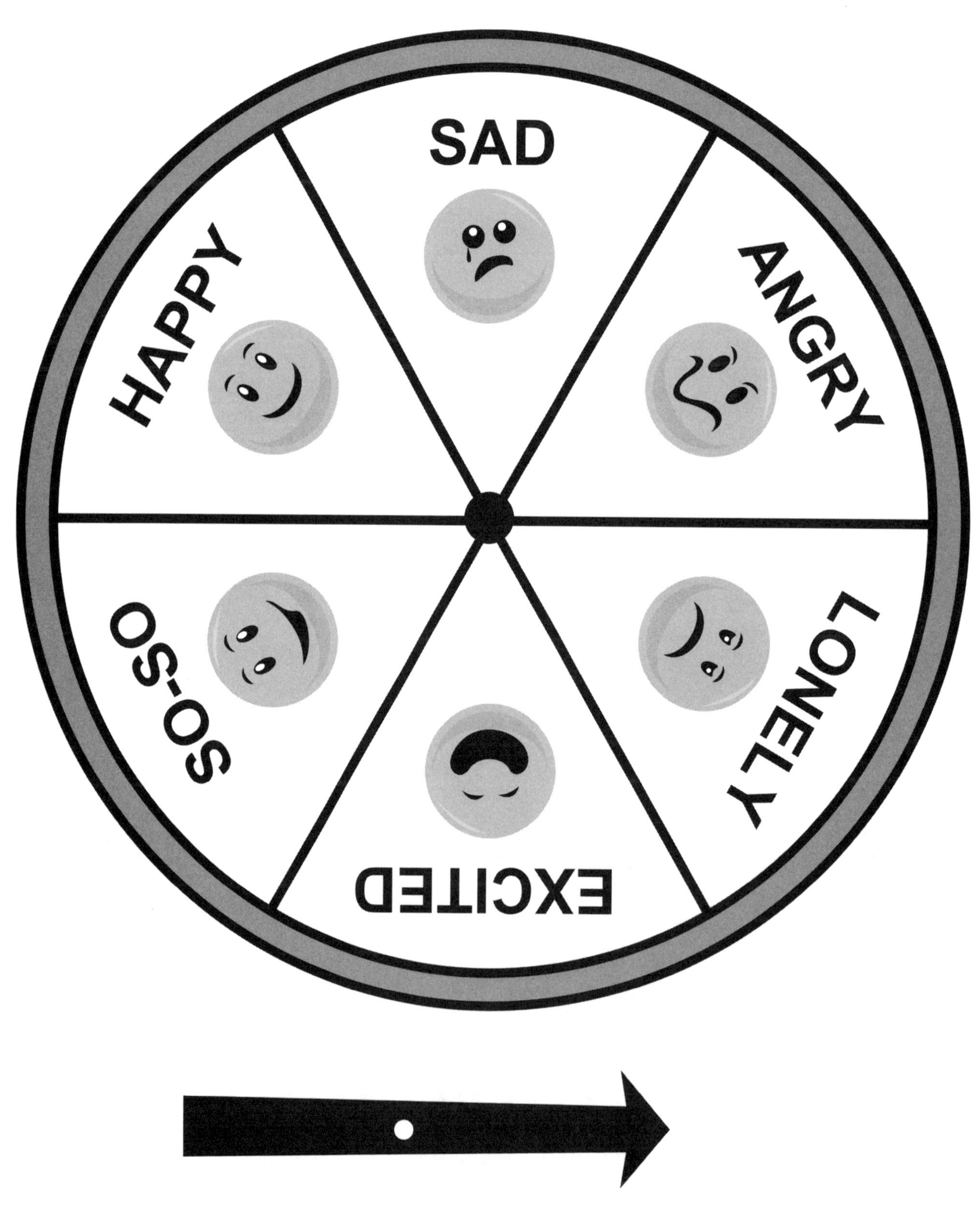

THE SMART FISH

This is the story of a fisherman who goes to the same spot every day to fish. He has been very successful in this spot and always catches a fish with the bait he uses.

One day, the fish began to think about what was happening.

At first, they wanted to bite the fisherman and hurt him like he was hurting them. But they realized that in order to do that, they would have to let him catch them. That would not be good.

They then looked more closely at the bait and saw a hook hidden in it.

"We must swim past the bait or surely we will be caught," the fish decided.

So when the fisherman dropped his baited line into the water as usual the next day, none of the fish would bite. This was very confusing to the fisherman! How could he be unable to catch a fish today when the same bait had always worked before?

The next day, the fisherman was determined to catch a fish so he put twice as much bait on the line. This was very tempting to the little fish, who thought this must be a feast. But just before biting into the tasty treat, they remembered about the hook and swam on by. Now the fisherman was really concerned!

"What is going on here?" he wanted to know.

The next day, the fisherman was more determined than ever to catch a fish. He put three times as much bait on the line. But the little fish were very smart and knew that the fisherman was only trying to catch them and eat them for dinner. They swam right by that beautiful bait.

The fisherman began to realize that the fish were onto his game and that he would have no more luck at that fishing hole. So he packed up his rod and reel and moved to a new fishing spot. The little fish were not bothered by him again.

When kids in class or on the bus tease and say mean things, they are trying to upset you and make you do something that will get you into trouble. They are being the fisherman. Sometimes the *bait* they use is very tempting. They may say things about your mother or you that are not nice. It is important that you realize that these things are not true and are not *meant* to be true. Just as the bait that the fisherman put on his line was not a true dinner for the little fish and was not meant to be.

When we give in to the anger we feel and say mean things back or hit or *get in someone's face*, the fisherman has *won*. We have been *caught!*

Only by being a *smart fish* and ignoring the bait can we escape the hook. When we first begin to ignore the mean words, the other kids are confused and are usually more determined to get us going. They will add more bait to the line. They will try even harder to catch us. But if we keep on ignoring the words, they will become tired, like the fisherman, and move on to a new person to bother. They may even stop fishing altogether!

Name ____ Grade ___________

CONTROLLING ANGER: ACTIVITY SHEET #1

Name ______________________________ Grade __________

FACT SHEET #1

People can control the anger they feel when others use mean words.

Session 3: Controlling Anger!
SITUATIONS CAN MAKE YOU ANGRY

Objective:

To help students learn to handle anger caused by disappointing, frustrating, or upsetting situations

Materials Needed:

For each student:

- ☑ *Anger Wheel* from Session 1
- ☑ *Feeling Wheel* from Session 2
- ☑ Copy of *Activity Sheet #2* (page 162)
- ☑ Copy of *Fact Sheet #2* (page 163)

For the leader:

- ☑ Students' folders
- ☑ Stickers
- ☑ Copy of *The Candle Of Friendship* (page 161)
- ☑ Cookie (optional)
- ☑ Candle (optional)
- ☑ Matches (optional)

Session Preparation:

Reproduce *Activity Sheet #2* and *Fact Sheet #2* for each student. Reproduce *The Candle Of Friendship* for the leader. Gather the other materials.

Session:

- Distribute the students' folders. Give each student a sticker to place on his/her folder cover.
- Have the students turn the pointer on their *Feeling Wheels* to indicate how they are feeling today. Allow those students who wish to do so to share their feelings with the group.
- Review the goals of the group.
- Explain that today the students will learn to handle anger caused by disappointing, frustrating or upsetting situations.
- Have the students review the information on their *Anger Wheels* and identify times they have been angry because they were disappointed or because something didn't go as they had planned.
- Explain that some adults get angry in heavy traffic because the cars aren't moving fast enough. Or they might get angry when they planned a picnic and it rained. These are situations that can lead to angry feelings. In these cases, people have the choice of continuing to be upset or changing the way they feel about the situation and moving on. Tell the students that the situations they feel angry about often involve sharing their friendships and feeling left out.
- Read *The Candle Of Caring*. (*Note:* The story is more effective if it is presented using a real cookie and a candle.)
- Distribute *Activity Sheet #2* to each student. Review the story's message about the cookie and the candle. Tell the students that if they keep telling themselves, "It's just not fair and I hate it," they will continue to feel angry. But if they change what they say to themselves, they can begin to feel better. It is like changing a CD in a CD player. They will continue to hear the same tune until they change the CD. They will continue to feel angry until they change the way they look at a situation.
- Distribute a copy of *Fact Sheet #2* to each student. Read the sentence and discuss it with the group.
- Have the students place their papers in their folders. Collect the folders.

THE CANDLE OF FRIENDSHIP

There was once a girl named Ann who had two friends. One of Ann's friends was named Sue and the other was named Gwen.

Sue liked to be with Ann, but she didn't want Ann to be friends with Gwen. Gwen liked to be with Ann, but she didn't want Ann to be friends with Sue!

Each girl was afraid that if Ann were friends with someone else, she wouldn't be friends with her any more. These girls thought friendship was like a cookie.

When you share a cookie with more and more people your piece gets smaller and smaller until finally, there may not be any cookie left! (If you are using a cookie, demonstrate by saying that the cookie is Ann. Break off a piece of the cookie and say that piece is Sue. Break off another piece and say that piece is Gwen. Illustrate how, as you break the pieces off, there is less of the cookie left. Just as Sue and Gwen thought there would be less left of Ann for them to have as a friend.)

Thank goodness friendship is *not* like a cookie! It is more like a *candle!*

(If you are using a candle, light it now.) When Ann sits at a table with a candle burning in the center, the light is bright as it shines on her. When Sue joins her at the table, the light shines just as brightly on Sue as it does on Ann. When Gwen joins Ann and Sue at the table, the light remains bright on Ann and Sue, but it shines just as brightly on Gwen! In fact, more and more friends could come to the table and the candlelight would shine on everyone equally.

We can have many friends at the same time. Being friends with one person does not mean that we cannot be friends with other people. Oh, and guess what? Each one of us has a *candle of friendship* within us. When we join with other people, we add our friendship light to the light of their candles, making an even brighter light for all of us to share. What a wonderful way to make a *bright future!*

Name ______________________________ Grade __________

CONTROLLING ANGER: ACTIVITY SHEET #2

Name ______________________________ Grade __________

FACT SHEET #2

People can control the anger they feel when things do not go as they planned.

Session 4: Controlling Anger!

HANDLING PHYSICAL ASSAULTS AND THREATS

Objective:

To help students learn to handle anger caused by physical assaults or threats

Materials Needed:

For each student:

- ☑ *Feeling Wheel* from previous session
- ☑ *Anger Wheel* from previous session
- ☑ Copy of *Activity Sheet #3* (page 165)
- ☑ Copy of *Rules For Solving Conflicts* (page 166)
- ☑ Copy of *Fact Sheet #3* (page 167)

For the leader:

- ☑ Students' folders
- ☑ Stickers

Session Preparation:

Reproduce *Rules For Solving Conflicts, Activity Sheet #3,* and *Fact Sheet #3* for each student. Gather the other materials.

Session:

- Distribute the students' folders. Give each student a sticker to place on his/her folder cover.
- Have the students turn the pointer on their *Feeling Wheels* to indicate how they are feeling today. Allow those students who wish to do so to share their feelings with the group.
- Review the goals of the group.
- Explain that today the students will learn to handle anger caused by threats or physical assaults—when someone hits, punches, kicks, or threatens to do any of those things.
- Have the students review the information on their *Anger Wheels* and identify times they have been angry because someone hurt them or threatened to hurt them.
- Distribute *Activity Sheet #3.* Explain that as conflicts escalate, they get more physical. Describe a situation in which a person threatens to hit someone and the person threatened responds by daring the other person to hit them. Continue showing how the situation becomes more and more intense until threats turn into physical action. Using the activity sheet, have the students tell, write, or act out ways they could stop the conflict from escalating.
- Explain the difference between *protecting oneself* and *fighting back.* It is OK to hold your hands up to protect your face or body. It is OK to hold someone's arm away from you if he/she tries to hit you. It is OK to call for help. It is OK to leave the immediate area when someone threatens you. It is NOT OK to hit back, kick, punch, or hurt the other person. This will NOT solve the problem. It will escalate the conflict.
- Distribute *Rules For Solving Conflicts* to each student. Review the rules and fouls aloud. Explain that when fouls are called in a sport, the player or team must pay a *penalty.* When people commit fouls in solving conflicts, the penalty is that the conflict escalates.
- Distribute a copy of *Fact Sheet #3.* Read the sentence and discuss it with the group.
- Have the students place their papers in their folders. Collect the folders.

Name ______________________________ Grade __________

CONTROLLING ANGER: ACTIVITY SHEET #3

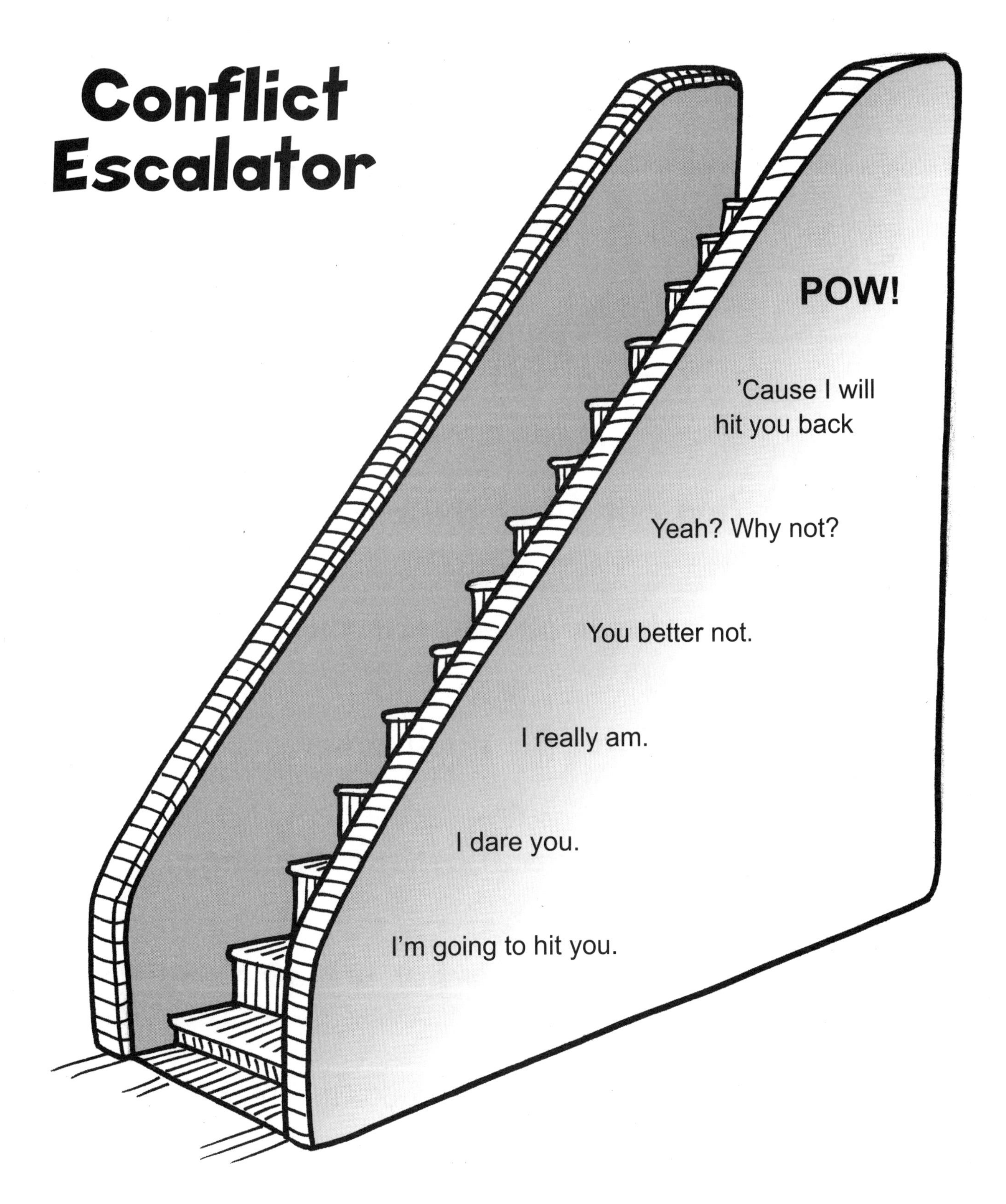

RULES FOR SOLVING CONFLICTS

~1~

We find out what the problem is.

~2~

We attack the problem, not the person.

~3~

We listen to each other.

~4~

We care about each other's feelings.

~5~

We are responsible for what we say and do.

Fouls: Hitting, biting, name-calling, put-downs, threats, teasing, blaming, not listening, getting even, bossing others

Name ______________________________________ Grade __________

FACT SHEET #3

People can control the anger they feel when others threaten them or hurt them.

Session 5: Controlling Anger!
RECOGNIZING THE HIDDEN FEELINGS OF ANGER

Objective:

To help students learn to recognize the hidden feelings behind anger

Materials Needed:

For each student:

- ☑ *Feeling Wheel* from previous session
- ☑ *Anger Wheel* from previous session
- ☑ Copy of *Activity Sheet #4* (page 170)
- ☑ Copy of *Fact Sheet #4* (page 171)
- ☑ Scissors
- ☑ Paintstick

For the leader:

- ☑ Students' folders
- ☑ Stickers
- ☑ Tagboard or cardstock
- ☑ Stapler and staples or gluestick

Session Preparation:

Reproduce *Activity Sheet #4* on tagboard or cardstock for each student. Reproduce *Fact Sheet #4* for each student. Gather the other necessary materials.

Session:

- Distribute the students' folders. Give each student a sticker to place on his/her folder cover.
- Have the students turn the pointer on their *Feeling Wheels* to indicate how they are feeling today. Allow those students who wish to do so to share their feelings with the group.
- Review the goals of the group.
- Explain that today the students will learn to recognize the feelings hidden behind anger. Use the following examples to show how anger is used as a *mask* to cover other uncomfortable feelings:

  When you fall down in class and everyone laughs, you feel embarrassed. Then you feel angry. (Your angry feelings are the mask for your embarrassment.)

  When you don't come home on time, your Mom feels scared. Then she becomes angry. (Your mom's angry feelings are the mask for being scared.)

  When your friends act like they don't want to play with you, you feel left out and you get angry. (Your angry feelings are the mask for feeling left out.)

  When it rains on a day you have big plans, you feel disappointed Then you feel angry. (Your angry feelings are a mask for being disappointed.)

- Explain that feelings of embarrassment, fear, being left out, disappointment, or loneliness, makes us all feel helpless and somewhat weak. Since these feelings make us very uncomfortable, we sometimes cover them with anger, because anger makes us feel strong and in control. In other words, we can take care of our angry feelings when we take care of the feelings hiding behind our anger.

- Distribute *Activity Sheet #4*, scissors, and a paintstick to each student. Tell the students to cut out the mask shape and eye holes.
- Glue or staple a paintstick to each mask.
- Have the students hold the masks up to their faces. Then have them pretend they are disappointed, left out, scared, and embarrassed.
- Explain that no matter how they were feeling behind the mask, all anyone saw on the outside was anger.
- Have the students review the information on the *Anger Wheel* and identify feelings that could be hiding behind anger in each instance.
- Distribute a copy of *Fact Sheet #4*. Read the sentence and discuss it with the group.
- Have the students place their papers in their folders.
- Collect the folders and any other materials that were distributed.

Name ______________________________________ Grade __________

CONTROLLING ANGER: ACTIVITY SHEET #4

Name ______________________________________ Grade __________

We can take care of the feelings that sometimes hide behind anger.

Session 6: Controlling Anger!
EXPRESSING ANGER IN CONSTRUCTIVE WAYS

Objective:

To help students learn to express anger in constructive ways

Materials Needed:

For each student:
- ☑ *Feeling Wheel* from previous session
- ☑ *Anger Wheel* from previous session
- ☑ Copy of *Activity Sheet #5A* (page 174)
- ☑ Copy of *Activity Sheet #5B* (page 175)
- ☑ Copy of *Fact Sheet #5* (page 176)
- ☑ Red, green, and yellow crayon
- ☑ Gluestick
- ☑ Scissors

For the leader:
- ☑ Students' folders
- ☑ Stickers
- ☑ Chalkboard and chalk or chart paper and marker

Session Preparation:

Reproduce *Activity Sheet #5A, Activity Sheet #5B,* and *Fact Sheet #5* for each student. Gather the other necessary materials.

Session:

- Distribute the students' folders. Give each student a sticker to place on his/her folder cover.
- Have the students turn the pointer on their *Feeling Wheels* to indicate how they are feeling today. Allow those students who wish to do so to share their feelings with the group.
- Review the goals of the group.
- Explain that today the students will learn to express their anger in helpful ways.
- Tell the students that people who are angry often do not take time to think. Instead, they do the first thing that pops into their heads. This is not a good idea, because everyone is responsible for the consequences of his/her actions, even if he/she is mad.
- Tell the students when they feel angry they should think of a traffic light. As you explain the following ideas to the students, write the meaning of each part of the traffic light on the board/chart paper.

  Red: Stop. Do nothing!

  Yellow: Breath, think, move slowly.

  Green: Choose a helpful thing to do!
- Distribute *Activity Sheet #5* and red, yellow, and green crayons to each student. Instruct the students to color the circles on their activity sheet red, yellow, and green; cut out the circles; and glue them to the traffic light.
- Discuss appropriate ways the students can react when they are angry. (Exercise, draw, write, punch a pillow, yell into a pillow, jump up and down, talk with friends, etc.)

- Have the students list, on the back of the traffic light, five or more positive actions they can perform when they are angry.
- Have the students review the information on the *Anger Wheel* and identify feelings that could be hiding behind anger in each instance.
- Distribute *Fact Sheet #4* to each student and discuss its message.
- Have the students place all their papers in their folders.
- Collect the folders for use in the next session. Collect any other materials that you distributed.

Name ______________________________ Grade __________

CONTROLLING ANGER: ACTIVITY SHEET #5A

Stop. Do nothing! RED

Breath, think, move slowly. YELLOW

Choose a helpful thing to do! GREEN

Name ____ Grade ___________

CONTROLLING ANGER: ACTIVITY SHEET #5B

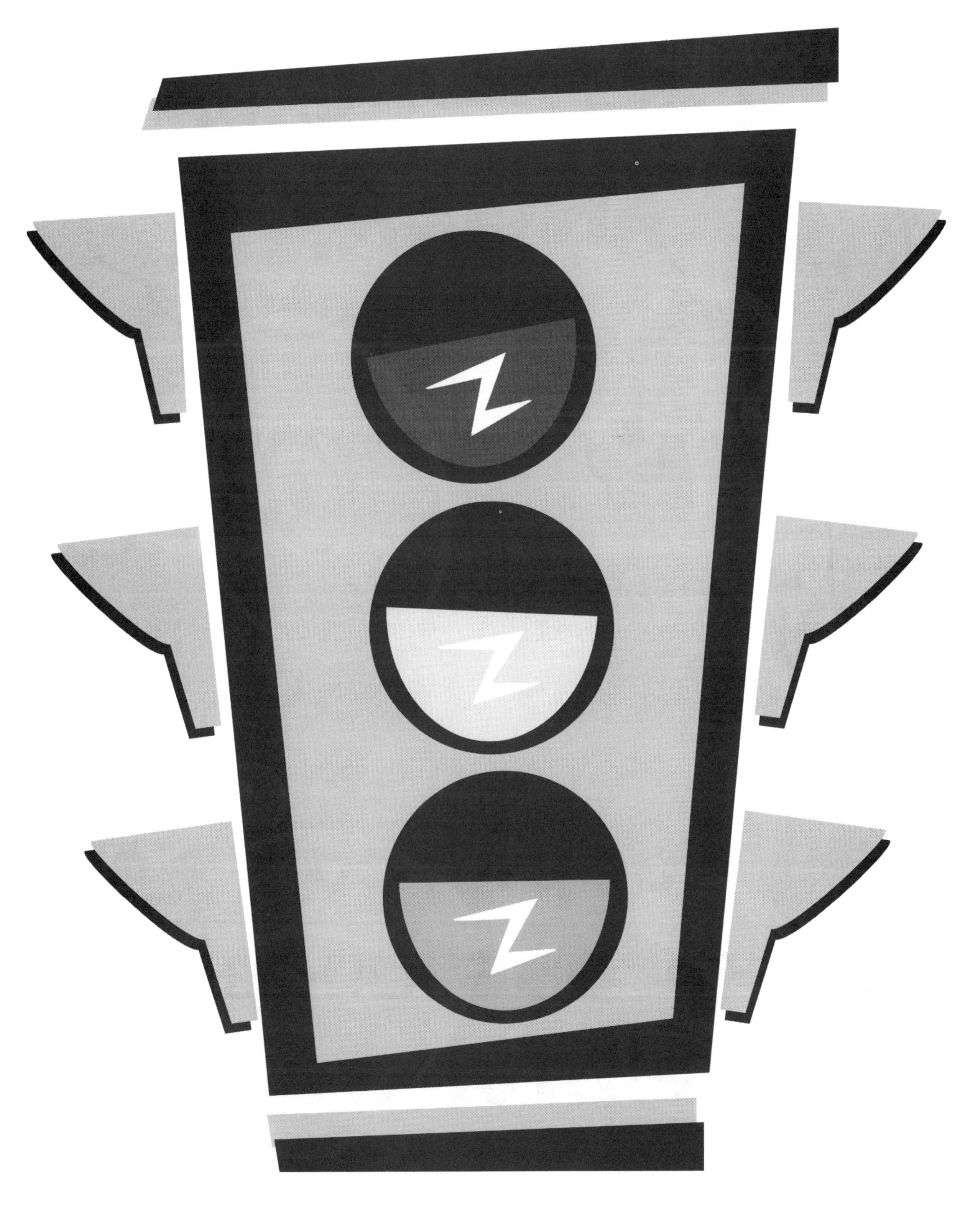

Name ________________________ Grade ________

People can express anger in helpful ways!

Session 7: Controlling Anger!
CONCLUSION

Objective:

To help students learn to celebrate controlling anger with positive actions

Materials Needed:

For each student:

☑ *Feeling Wheel* from previous session
☑ Copy of *Evaluation Sheet* (page 178)
☑ Pencil

For the leader:

☑ Students' folders
☑ Stickers
☑ Copy of *The Smart Fish* (page 157)
☑ Copy of *The Candle Of Friendship* (page 161)
☑ Refreshments (optional)

Session Preparation:

Reproduce an *Evaluation Sheet* for each student. Gather the other necessary materials.

Session:

- Distribute the students' folders. Give each student a sticker to place on his/her folder cover.
- Have the students turn the pointer on their *Feeling Wheels* to indicate how they are feeling today. Allow those students who wish to do so to share their feelings with the group.
- Review the goals of the group.
- Explain that today the students will celebrate the fact that they can use positive actions to control their anger.
- Review *The Smart Fish* story. Emphasize that this is the story that taught the students what to do when people say mean things. Ask the students what they should do when someone says mean things to them. (Ignore what was said and walk away.)
- Review *The Candle Of Friendship* story. Ask the students what they learned from the cookies and the candle. (Friendship is not like a cookie. When you share a cookie, it becomes smaller and smaller. Friendship is like a candle. It stays bright and shining, no matter how many friends you have.)
- Review the significance of the CD player. (Unless you change the CD in the player, you will always hear the same tune. Unless you change yourselves when you are angry, you will always feel the same way.)
- Review the significance of the *Conflict Escalator*. (Conflicts will climb like an escalator, going up unless the students know and use ways to stop the escalator and stop the conflict.)
- Review the significance of the *Anger Mask*. (Angry feelings sometimes hide other feelings that we should deal with.)
- Review the significance of the *Traffic Light*. (The traffic light taught the steps for dealing with anger in a positive way.)
- Distribute an *Evaluation Sheet* and a pencil to each student. Have the students complete the evaluation. (*Note:* You may wish to serve refreshments at this time.)
- Collect the *Evaluation Sheets*.
- Collect any materials that you distributed. Thank the students for their cooperation and give them their folders to take home.

CONTROLLING ANGER
EVALUATION SHEET

Name ______________________________ Grade _____

One thing I learned in this group was ________________

____

____

____.

The best part of the group was ________________________

____

____

____.

One thing I would change about the group is __________

____

____

____.

UNDERSTANDING SELF & OTHERS

The Me Beyond The Mirror: Self-Esteem (Grades 1-3)
by Kaye Aguirre

Shy Or Withdrawn Students (Grades 1-3)

I'm Special (Grades K-2)

Friendship (Grades 1-3)

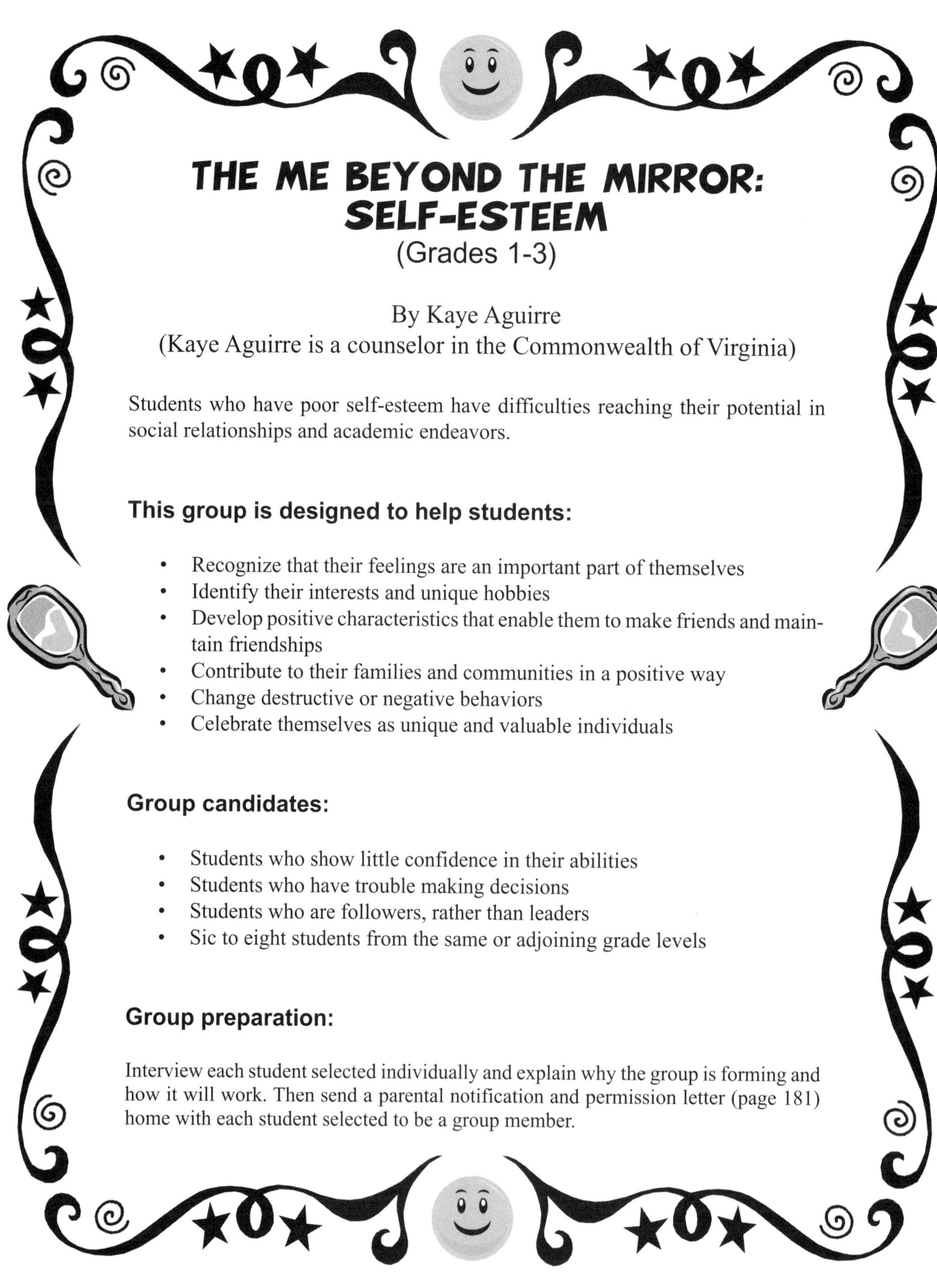

THE ME BEYOND THE MIRROR: SELF-ESTEEM

(Grades 1-3)

By Kaye Aguirre
(Kaye Aguirre is a counselor in the Commonwealth of Virginia)

Students who have poor self-esteem have difficulties reaching their potential in social relationships and academic endeavors.

This group is designed to help students:

- Recognize that their feelings are an important part of themselves
- Identify their interests and unique hobbies
- Develop positive characteristics that enable them to make friends and maintain friendships
- Contribute to their families and communities in a positive way
- Change destructive or negative behaviors
- Celebrate themselves as unique and valuable individuals

Group candidates:

- Students who show little confidence in their abilities
- Students who have trouble making decisions
- Students who are followers, rather than leaders
- Sic to eight students from the same or adjoining grade levels

Group preparation:

Interview each student selected individually and explain why the group is forming and how it will work. Then send a parental notification and permission letter (page 181) home with each student selected to be a group member.

Dear ____:

As part of the guidance program, it is my privilege to provide opportunities for students to meet in small groups. The purpose of these groups is to allow the students to acquire information and skills that will help them become more successful in the school setting. School success depends not only on academic ability, but also on self-confidence and social adjustment.

Your child has an opportunity to participate in a group called *The Me Beyond The Mirror*. This group is designed to help students recognize the interests, hobbies, and abilities that make them unique and important individuals with strong connections to their families, friends, school, and communities.

Each of the seven group meetings will last approximately 30-minutes. The meetings will be held at a time the classroom teacher selects.

Your child knows about the group and has indicated that he or she would like to participate in it. However, no child is ever included in a small-group counseling program without his or her parents' knowledge and permission.

Please indicate, by completing the form below, that you wish to have your child participate in this group or that you do not want him or her to be included.

Return the permission slip to me by ________________________.

Thank you,

✂- -

☐ I, ______________________________, ***give permission*** for my child to participate in the small-group counseling program on self-confidence.

☐ I, ______________________________, ***do not give permission*** for my child to participate in the small-group counseling program on self-confidence.

Child's Name ______________________________ Date ____________

School ______________________________ Grade ____________

Teacher ______________________________

Home Phone (____) ____________ Work Phone (____) ____________

Parent's Printed Name ______________________________

Parent's Signature ______________________________

Session 1: Self-Esteem
INTRODUCTION

Objective:

To introduce the students to each other and teach them the goals and rules of the group

Materials Needed:

For each student:

- ☑ Copy of *The Me Beyond The Mirror Goals* (page 183)
- ☑ Copy of *The Me Beyond The Mirror Rules* (page 184)
- ☑ Copy of *The Me Beyond The Mirror Folder Cover* (page 185)
- ☑ Piece of construction paper
- ☑ Gluestick
- ☑ Pencil
- ☑ Crayons or marker

For the leader:

- ☑ Dice
- ☑ Instant camera and film

Session Preparation:

Reproduce *The Me Beyond The Mirror Goals, The Me Beyond The Mirror Rules*, and *The Me Beyond The Mirror Folder Cover* for each student. Gather the other necessary materials.

Session:

- Introduce yourself to the group.
- Have the group members introduce themselves to each other by rolling the dice and telling one fact about themselves for each number shown on the dice.
- Distribute *The Me Beyond The Mirror Goals, The Me Beyond The Mirror Rules, The Me Beyond The Mirror Folder Cover,* construction paper, a gluestick, a pencil, and crayons or markers to each student. Have the students fold the construction paper in half.
- Review *The Me Beyond The Mirror Goals.* Explain that the group will meet every week for seven weeks.
- Review *The Me Beyond The Mirror Rules.* Have each student sign his/her name on the line provided if he/she agrees to follow the rules and is interested in remaining in the group.
- Have the students look at *The Me Beyond The Mirror Folder Cover.* Explain that in this group, they will be learning about their "inside" selves and the things that make them special.
- Photograph each student and have the students glue their pictures in the "mirror" on the cover sheet. Have them put their names on *The Me Beyond The Mirror Folder Cover*, then glue the folder cover to the construction paper. Allow time for the students to decorate their covers.
- Have the students place *The Me Beyond The Mirror Goals* and *The Me Beyond The Mirror Rules* in their folders. Collect the folders and any other distributed materials.

GOALS

In this group I will:

1
Learn about my feelings.

2
Identify activities that I enjoy.

3
Learn about the characteristics that help me make and keep friends.

4
Develop skills that help me help others.

5
Learn how to make changes in my behavior when necessary.

6
Celebrate my uniqueness!

THE ME BEYOND THE MIRROR

RULES
1
I will respect the privacy of others.
2
I will wait my turn to speak.
3
I will listen when others speak.
4
I will keep my hands to myself.
5
I will come to group meetings
and be on time.
6
I will be responsible for
class work missed due to
group meetings.
THE ME BEYOND THE MIRROR
SIGNATURE
DATE

The
ME
Beyond
The Mirror
Name

Session 2: Self-Esteem
IDENTIFYING FEELINGS

Objective:

To help students recognize their feelings and realize how important their feelings are

Materials Needed:

For each student:
- ☑ Copy of *Activity Sheet #1* (page 188)
- ☑ Copy of *Fact Sheet #1* (page 189)
- ☑ Folder
- ☑ Pencil

For the leader:
- ☑ Stickers
- ☑ Mirror

Session Preparation:

Reproduce *Fact Sheet #1* and *Activity Sheet #1* for each student. Gather the other necessary materials.

Session:

- Distribute the folders to the group members. Give each student a sticker to place on the cover of his/her *The Me Beyond The Mirror Folder.*

- Introduce the session by telling the students that their feelings are a part of them, just as their eyes, noses, or hands. The only difference is that they can see their hands, noses, and eyes, but they cannot see their feelings.

- Pass the mirror in front of each student. Explain that the way we feel about things helps us know what we like and what we don't like. The way we feel about things also helps us to know how to be safe and how to have fun. Even though our feelings are inside of us and we cannot see them, we often show feelings as facial expressions. It is like an artist who draws bending trees to show wind. We cannot see the wind, but we know what the artist means. We use facial expressions in the same way.

- Pass the mirror around and have each student show a happy face in the mirror. Do the same with about three other feelings, such as anger, sadness, and fright. Discuss each feeling expressed and identify situations that could cause these feelings to occur. Then ask:

  Does everyone feel the same when things happen? (No. If you need an example to make this clear, ask how many of the students like broccoli. If everyone likes broccoli, continue until you find something they do not all agree on. Then ask how they feel when they have to eat broccoli or whatever thing you have chosen.)

  Is it possible to have more than one feeling at a time? (Yes. If you need an example to make this clear, ask the students how they would feel if they were invited to an amusement park. Then ask them how they would feel it they were told they were going to ride an especially large roller coaster or go into an especially scary haunted house display. They might be excited to go to the amusement park and a little bit scared of the ride or the haunted house.)

- Distribute *Fact Sheet #1, Activity Sheet #1,* and a pencil to each student. Discuss the sentences on *Fact Sheet #1.*

- Read descriptions of the following situations. After reading each situation, have the students draw a facial expression on *Activity Sheet #1* showing how a person in that situation might feel and record the feeling expressed on the line below the circle.

  1. *How might a person feel who just tripped and fell in front of the class?*
  2. *How might a person feel if he or she was going to sing a solo in the school play?*
  3. *How might a person feel when his or her pet is sick?*
  4. *How might a person feel when it is his or her birthday?*
  5. *How might a person feel when he or she is alone in the house?*

- Have the students share their completed drawings with the group.

- Conclude the lesson by explaining that some feelings—like loneliness, embarrassment, and rejection—make us uncomfortable. Explain that even though these feelings make us uncomfortable, they can help us make changes in ourselves. This is because *we* are in control of how we feel and only *we* can change the way we feel by changing the way we view the situation.

- Have the students write their name and grade on both activity sheets and place them in their folders. Collect the folders and any other distributed materials.

Name ______________________________ Grade __________

THE ME BEYOND THE MIRROR

ACTIVITY SHEET #1

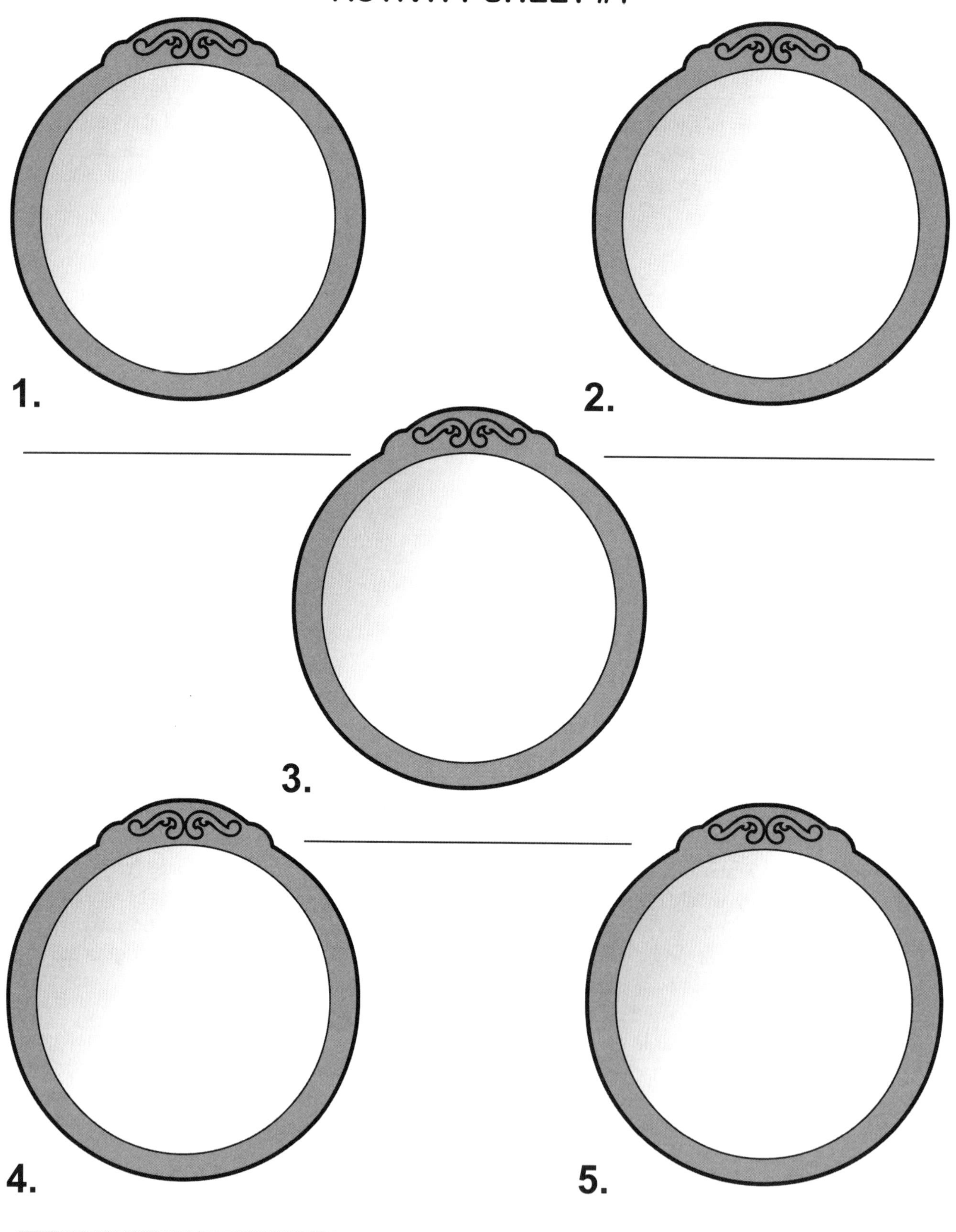

FACT SHEET #1
My feelings
are part of me.
My feelings are
important and they
can help me!
THE ME BEYOND THE MIRROR
NAME
GRADE

Session 3: Self-Esteem
INTERESTS EFFECT CHOICES

Objective:

To have students identify their interests and learn how their interests affect the friends they choose and the way they spend their time

Materials Needed:

For each student:

- ☑ Copy of *Activity Sheet #2* (page 191)
- ☑ Copy of *Fact Sheet #2* (page 192)
- ☑ Folder
- ☑ Magazines
- ☑ Glue
- ☑ Scissors

For the leader:

- ☑ Stickers
- ☑ Mirror

Session Preparation:

Reproduce *Fact Sheet #2* and *Activity Sheet #2* for each student. Gather the other necessary materials.

Session:

- Distribute the folders to the group members. Give each student a sticker to place on the cover of his/her *The Me Beyond The Mirror Folder.*
- Sclcct two students for a demonstration. Give the mirror to one student. Ask that student to think of a favorite food and look into the mirror. Ask the other student to look at the image in the mirror and name that person's favorite food. When he/she cannot name the other student's favorite food, explain that although interests and hobbies may not show up when we look in a mirror, they are important because they help determine who our friends will be, how we spend our time, and how we make decisions. Have the students return to their seats.
- Have the students name their favorite foods, TV shows, books, music, sports, etc. Then ask several students:

  How does your favorite TV show help you decide how to use your time?

  How does your favorite sport help you decide whom you would like for a friend?

- Distribute *Activity Sheet #2, Fact Sheet #2,* magazines, scissors, and glue to the students. Begin by discussing the sentences on *Fact Sheet #2.*
- Tell the students to cut out pictures from the magazines that show things they are interested in, hobbies, or favorite foods, TV shows, clothing styles, etc. They should then glue their pictures onto the bag on *Activity Sheet #2.* Have the students share their completed activity sheets with the group.
- Have the students write their name and grade on both activity sheets and place them in their folders. Collect the folders and any other distributed materials.

Name ________________________________ Grade __________

THE ME BEYOND THE MIRROR

ACTIVITY SHEET #2

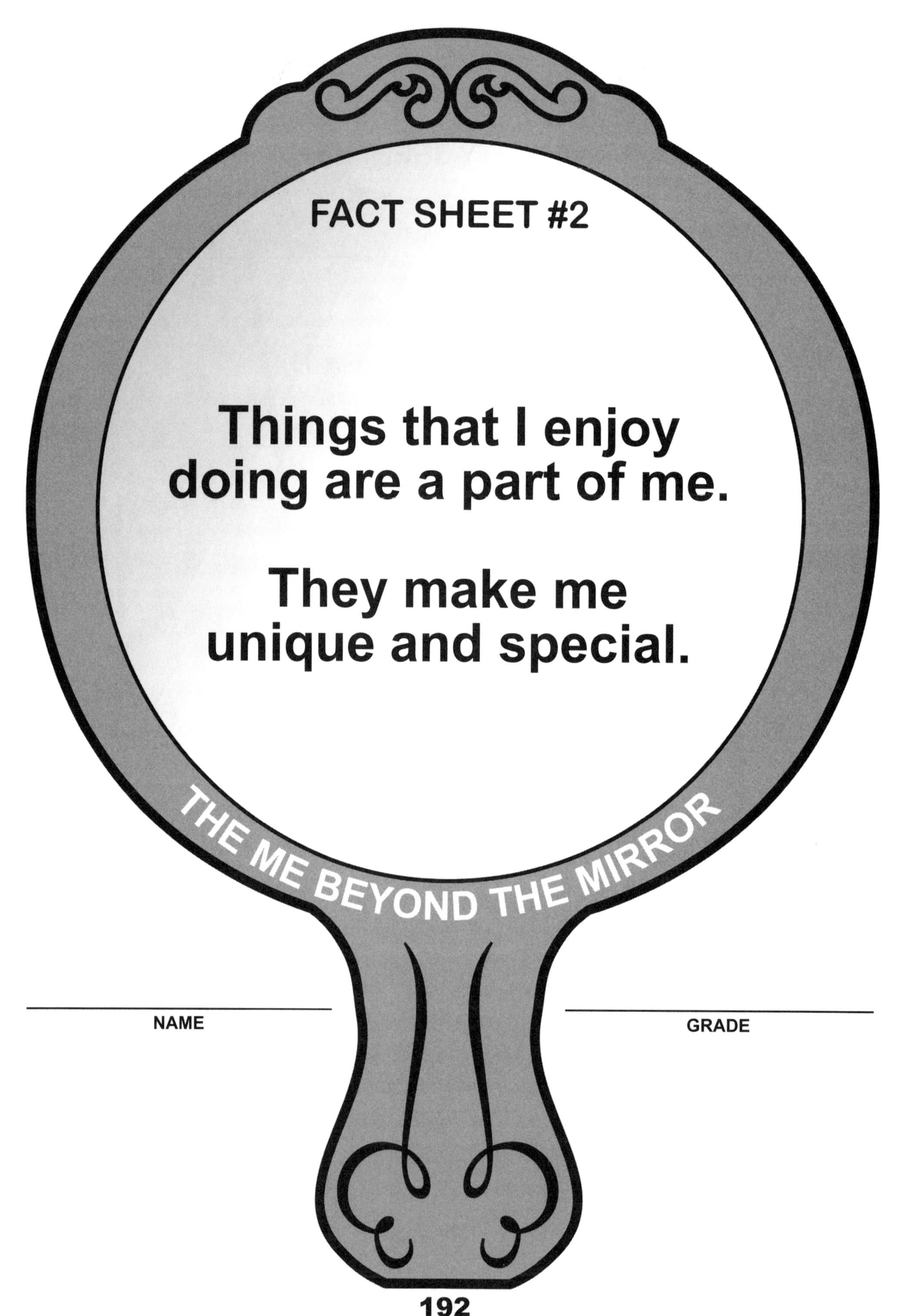
FACT SHEET #2
Things that I enjoy doing are a part of me.
They make me unique and special.
THE ME BEYOND THE MIRROR
NAME
GRADE

Session 4: Self-Esteem
POSITIVE QUALITIES

Objective:

To help students identify the positive qualities that make them good friends

Materials Needed:

For each student:

☑ Copy of *Activity Sheet #3* (page 194)
☑ Copy of *Fact Sheet #3* (page 195)
☑ Folder
☑ Pencil

For the leader:

☑ Stickers

Session Preparation:

Reproduce *Fact Sheet #3* and *Activity Sheet #3* for each student. Gather the other necessary materials.

Session:

- Distribute the folders to the group members. Give each student a sticker to place on the cover of his/her *The Me Beyond The Mirror Folder.*
- Review the facts the students learned in the previous two sessions. Remind the students that their feelings and interests are important parts of them but are not always visible in the mirror. Explain that they possess other qualities that are not visible, either. These are traits that other people admire and notice as "friendship qualities."
- Have the students brainstorm qualities they admire in their friends and in other people. Then have them identify characteristics of their own that others find friendly. Then ask:

  What do your true friends like about you?

- Distribute *Fact Sheet #3, Activity Sheet #3,* and a pencil to each student. Discuss the sentence on *Fact Sheet #3.*
- Have the students look at *Activity Sheet #3.* Review, with the students, the characteristics listed at the bottom of the page. Discuss how each of these qualities is very important in making and keeping friends. Then have the students complete the word puzzle.
- Have the students write their name and grade on both activity sheets and place them in their folders. Collect the folders and any other distributed materials.

Name ______________________________ Grade __________

THE ME BEYOND THE MIRROR

ACTIVITY SHEET #3

A	C	E	G	I	D	K	I	N	D	P
Z	W	C	A	R	I	N	G	S	V	J
I	M	A	G	I	N	A	T	I	O	N
B	D	F	H	J	L	N	P	R	T	V
R	R	E	S	P	E	C	T	L	C	Q
K	I	K	N	H	E	L	P	F	U	L
C	R	E	A	T	I	V	E	P	Q	C
D	G	H	L	O	U	G	H	C	S	R
N	D	T	H	U	M	O	R	C	E	E
K	G	E	N	E	R	O	U	S	P	S

WORD LIST:

HELPFUL
KIND
CARING
GENEROUS
CREATIVE
IMAGINATION
HUMOR
RESPECT

FACT SHEET #3
Things that I do and
the way I treat others
can help me make
and keep friends.
THE ME BEYOND THE MIRROR
NAME
GRADE

Session 5: Self-Esteem
CARING ABOUT THE COMMUNITY

Objective:

To help students identify ways to show caring attitudes in their communities

Materials Needed:

For each student:

- ☑ Copy of *Activity Sheet #4* (page 198)
- ☑ Copy of *Fact Sheet #4* (page 199)
- ☑ Folder
- ☑ Pencil

For the leader:

- ☑ Stickers
- ☑ Chalkboard and chalk or chart paper and marker
- ☑ *Circles Of Caring* (page 200)

Session Preparation:

Reproduce *Fact Sheet #4* and *Activity Sheet #4* for each student. Using *Circles of Caring* as a pattern, draw a large version on the board/chart paper. Gather the other necessary materials.

Session:

- Distribute the folders to the group members. Give each student a sticker to place on the cover of his/her *The Me Beyond The Mirror Folder.*
- Review the facts discussed in the previous sessions. Explain that just as feelings, interests, and friendly attitudes are not always visible in the mirror, students' connection to their families and communities in an important non-visible part of their character.
- Ask the students to look at the enlarged copy of *Circles Of Caring* on the board/chart paper. Then:

  Point to the *Self* circle. Tell the students that when they were newborn babies, the only person they knew or cared about was themselves.

  Point to the *Parents* circle. Tell the students that as they grew, they began to connect with and care about their parents, too.

  Point to the *Brothers and Sisters* circle. Tell the students that as they became older, the circle might have grown to include brothers and sisters.

  Point to the *Extended Family* circle. Tell the students that their circle might have grown to include grandparents, uncles, aunts, cousins, and other relatives.

  Point to the *Friends and Neighbors* circle. Tell the students that as they grew older, the circle grew larger and included friends and neighbors.

  Point to the *Community* circle. Tell the students that when they went to school, the circle became larger and grew to include classmates. Emphasize that as they continue to grow, the circle will grow. Explain that connections to other people are a very important part of each of us.

- Distribute *Fact Sheet #4, Activity Sheet #4,* and a pencil to each student. Discuss the sentences on *Fact Sheet #4.*

- Have the students look at *Activity Sheet #4.* Tell the students that more people can be included in the community circle. Discuss those people in the community whom the students may feel are their friends or associates. Write the names of these people on the board/chart paper. Then brainstorm ways the students can show a caring attitude toward these people. If the postal worker is named, for example, the students may say they can be polite and make sure their mailbox is emptied each day. When the group has finished brainstorming, have the students write on *Activity Sheet #4* ways they can show a caring attitude to people in their communities.

- Have the students write their name and grade on the activity sheets and place them in their folders. Collect the folders and any other distributed materials.

Name ______________________________ Grade __________

THE ME BEYOND THE MIRROR

ACTIVITY SHEET #4

FACT SHEET #4
Helping my family, friends, and community is important.
It makes me feel good about myself.
THE ME BEYOND THE MIRROR
NAME
GRADE

Name ______________________________ Grade __________

CIRCLES OF CARING

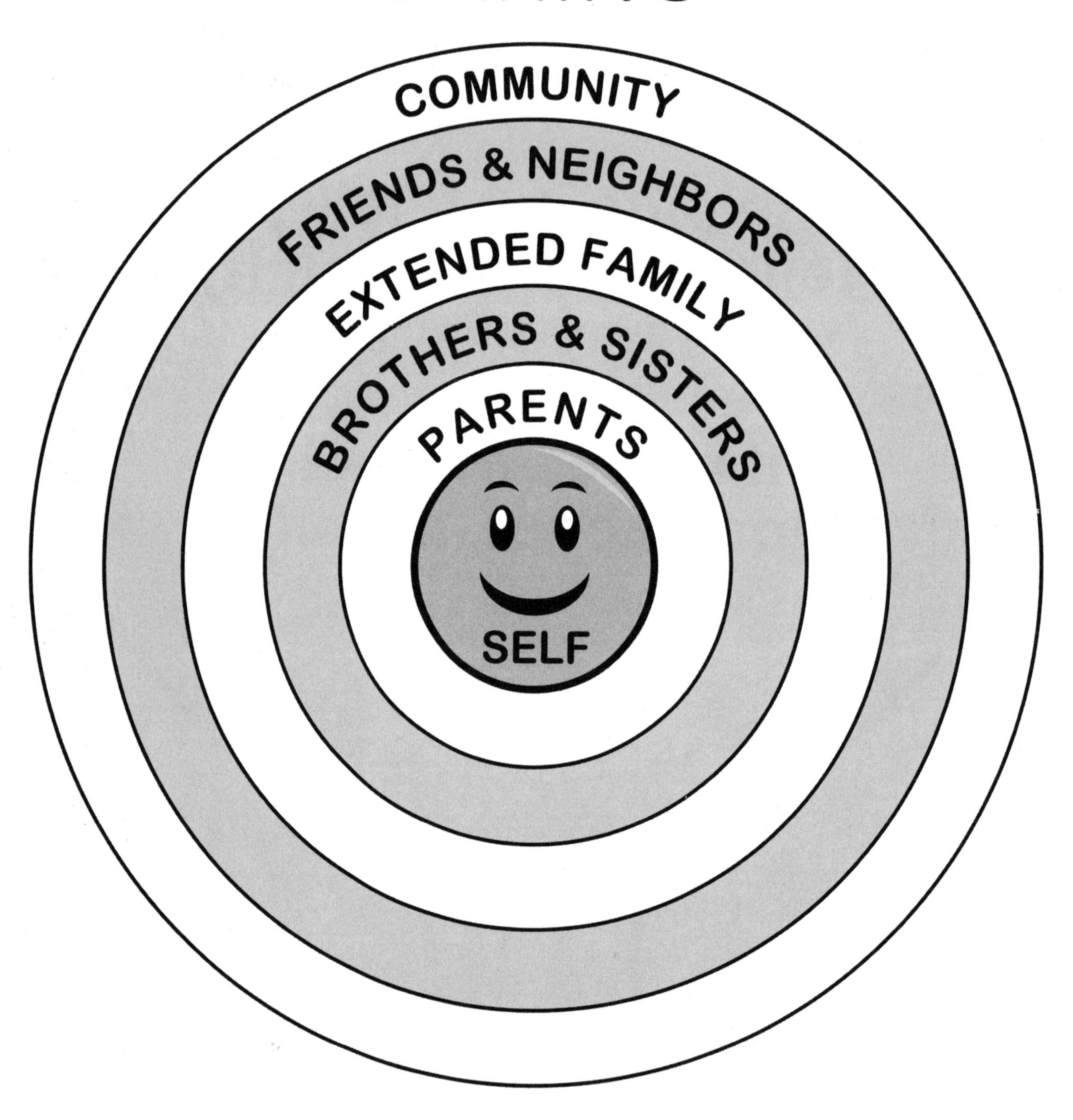

Session 6: Self-Esteem
MAKING CHANGES

Objective:

To help students identify things about themselves that they would like to change

Materials Needed:

For each student:
- ☑ Copy of *Activity Sheet #5* (page 202)
- ☑ Copy of *Fact Sheet #5* (page 203)
- ☑ Folder
- ☑ Pencil

For the leader:
- ☑ Stickers

Session Preparation:

Reproduce *Fact Sheet #5* and *Activity Sheet #5* for each student. Gather the other necessary materials.

Session:

- Distribute the folders to the group members. Give each student a sticker to place on the cover of his/her *The Me Beyond The Mirror Folder.*
- Review the concepts discussed during the previous sessions. Explain that the students have identified many positive and important parts of themselves that are not always visible in the mirror. Tell them that no one is perfect and that there may be things about themselves they would like to change or improve. Examples could include improving academically, having more friends, etc. Let the students know they can make changes in themselves by making the appropriate decisions.
- Have the students brainstorm decisions they could make that would help them be more successful in their schoolwork.
- Distribute *Fact Sheet #5* to each student. Discuss the sentences on it.
- Distribute *Activity Sheet #5* and a pencil to each student. Have the students brainstorm areas they would like to change in themselves, then list those areas on their activity sheet.
- Have the students brainstorm decisions they would need to make or actions they would need to take to make these changes occur, then write those decisions or actions on their activity sheet.
- Have the students write their name and grade on both activity sheets and place them in their folders. Collect the folders.

Name ________________________ Grade __________

THE ME BEYOND THE MIRROR

ACTIVITY SHEET #5

THINGS I WOULD LIKE TO CHANGE	WAY I CAN CHANGE
________________	________________
________________	________________
________________	________________
________________	________________
________________	________________
________________	________________
________________	________________
________________	________________
________________	________________
________________	________________
________________	________________
________________	________________

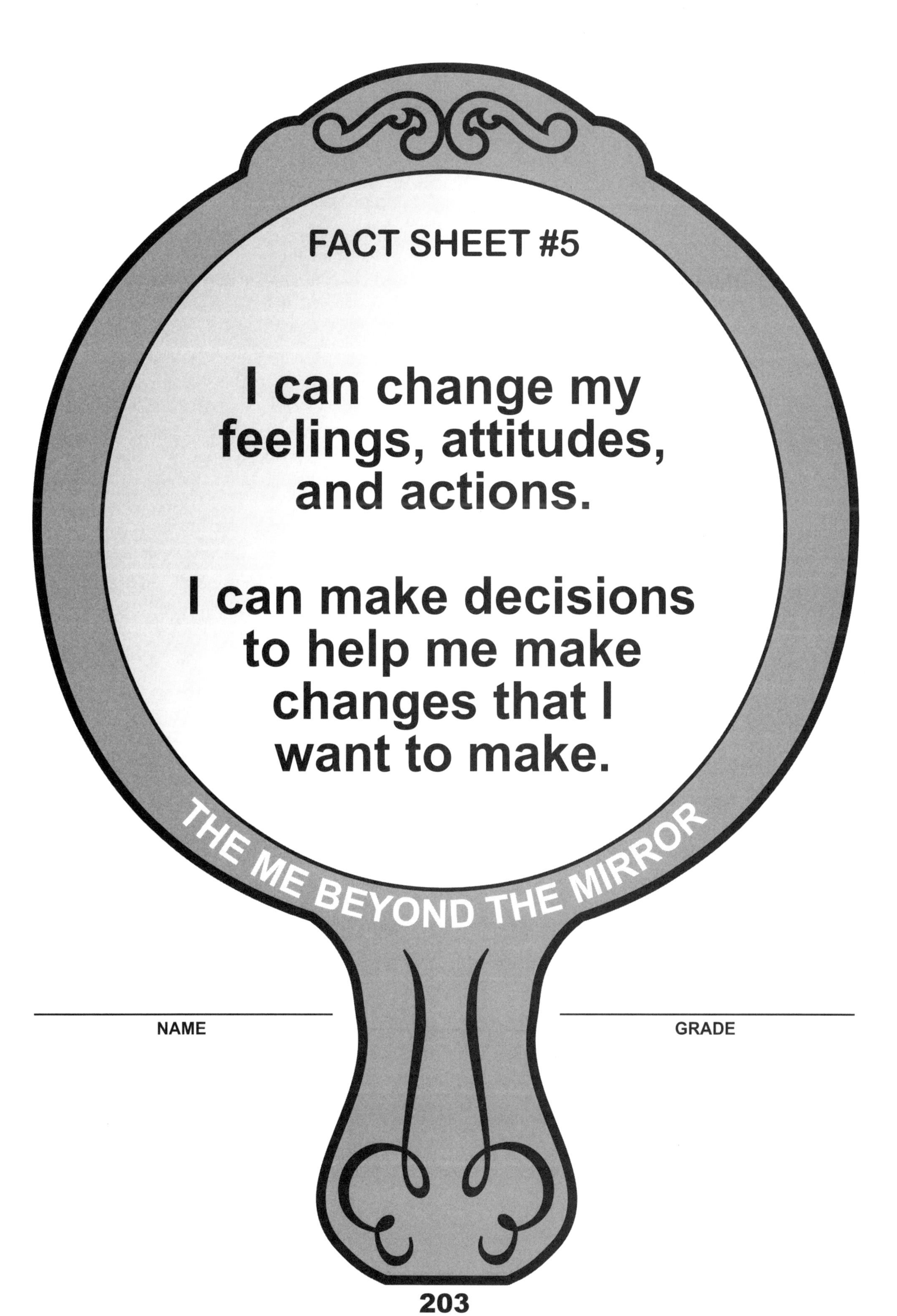
FACT SHEET #5
I can change my feelings, attitudes, and actions.
I can make decisions to help me make changes that I want to make.
THE ME BEYOND THE MIRROR
NAME
GRADE

Session 7: Self-Esteem
THE ME BEYOND THE MIRROR

Objective:

To encourage students to celebrate their uniqueness

Materials Needed:

For each student:

- ☑ Copy of *Activity Sheet #6* (page 205)
- ☑ Copy of *Fact Sheet #6* (page 206)
- ☑ Copy of *"ME" Poster* (page 207)
- ☑ Folder
- ☑ Pencil
- ☑ Crayons or markers

For the leader:

- ☑ Stickers
- ☑ Access to soap and water
- ☑ Stamp pad
- ☑ Refreshments (optional)

Session Preparation:

Reproduce *Fact Sheet #6, Activity Sheet #6, and "ME" Poster* for each student. Gather the other necessary materials.

Session:

- Distribute the folders to the group members. Give each student a sticker to place on the cover of his/her *The Me Beyond The Mirror Folder.*
- Review the facts the students learned in the previous sessions. Explain that each group member is unique and special on the outside and on the inside. No two people, even twins, are exactly alike.
- Distribute *Activity Sheet #6.* Have each student use the stamp pad to make a handprint on his/her activity sheet. Then have the students compare handprints and tell how theirs are alike and different from those of other students in the group. (*Note:* Be sure to have each student wash his/her hands after making the handprint.)
- Distribute *Fact Sheet #6* to each student and discuss the sentences on it.
- Distribute a *"ME" Poster*, a pencil, and crayons or markers to each student. Have the students complete the poster by drawing and decorating the required pictures. If time allows, have the students share their posters with the group. (*Note:* While the students complete their posters, refreshments may be served.)
- Thank the students for their cooperation during these sessions. Have the students write their name and grade on the activity sheets and place them in their folders. Allow the students to take their folders home with them.

Name ____ Grade ___________

THE ME BEYOND THE MIRROR

ACTIVITY SHEET #6

My Handprint
Is Unique

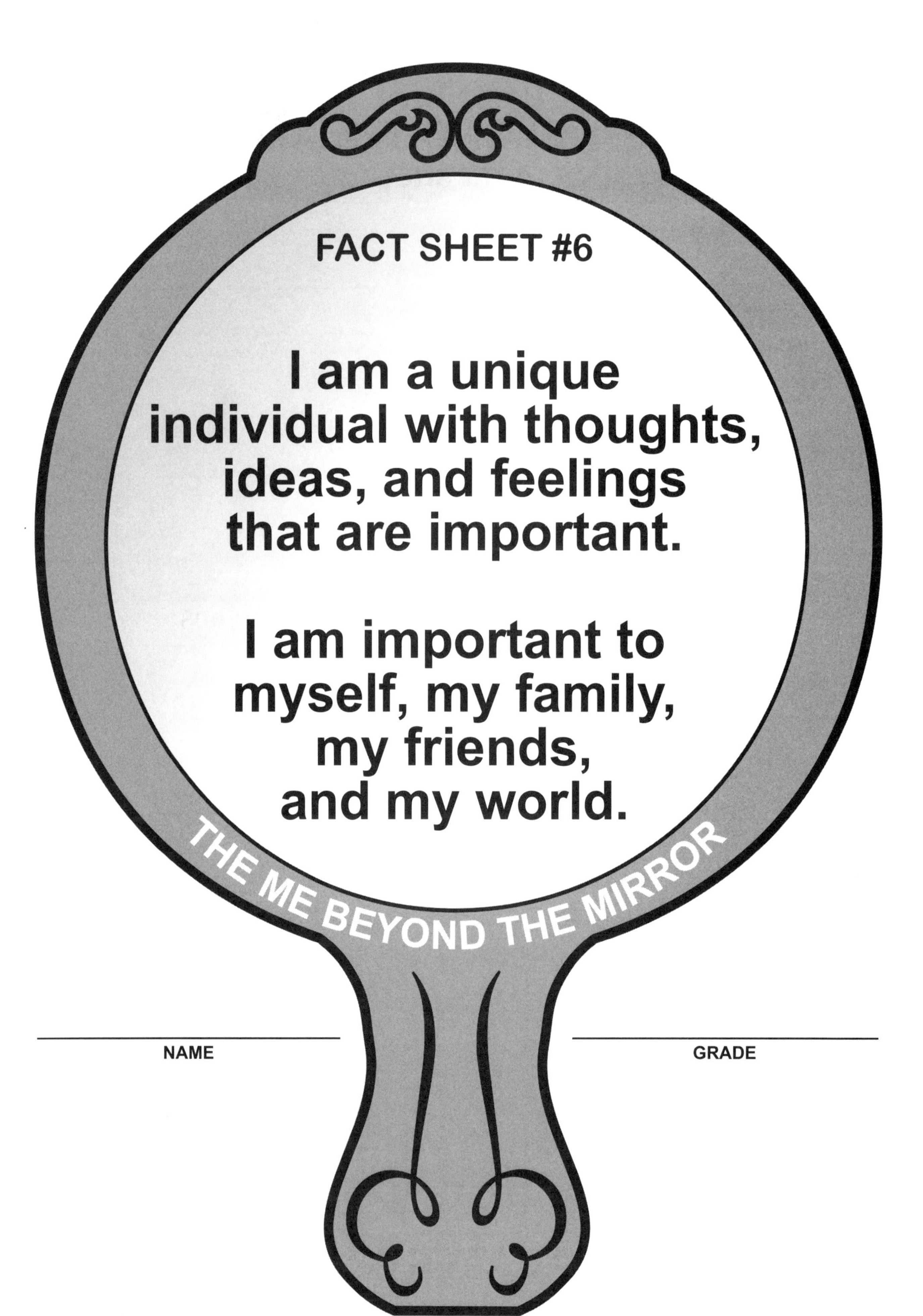
FACT SHEET #6
I am a unique individual with thoughts, ideas, and feelings that are important.
I am important to myself, my family, my friends, and my world.
THE ME BEYOND THE MIRROR
NAME
GRADE

Name ______________________________ Grade __________

"ME" POSTER

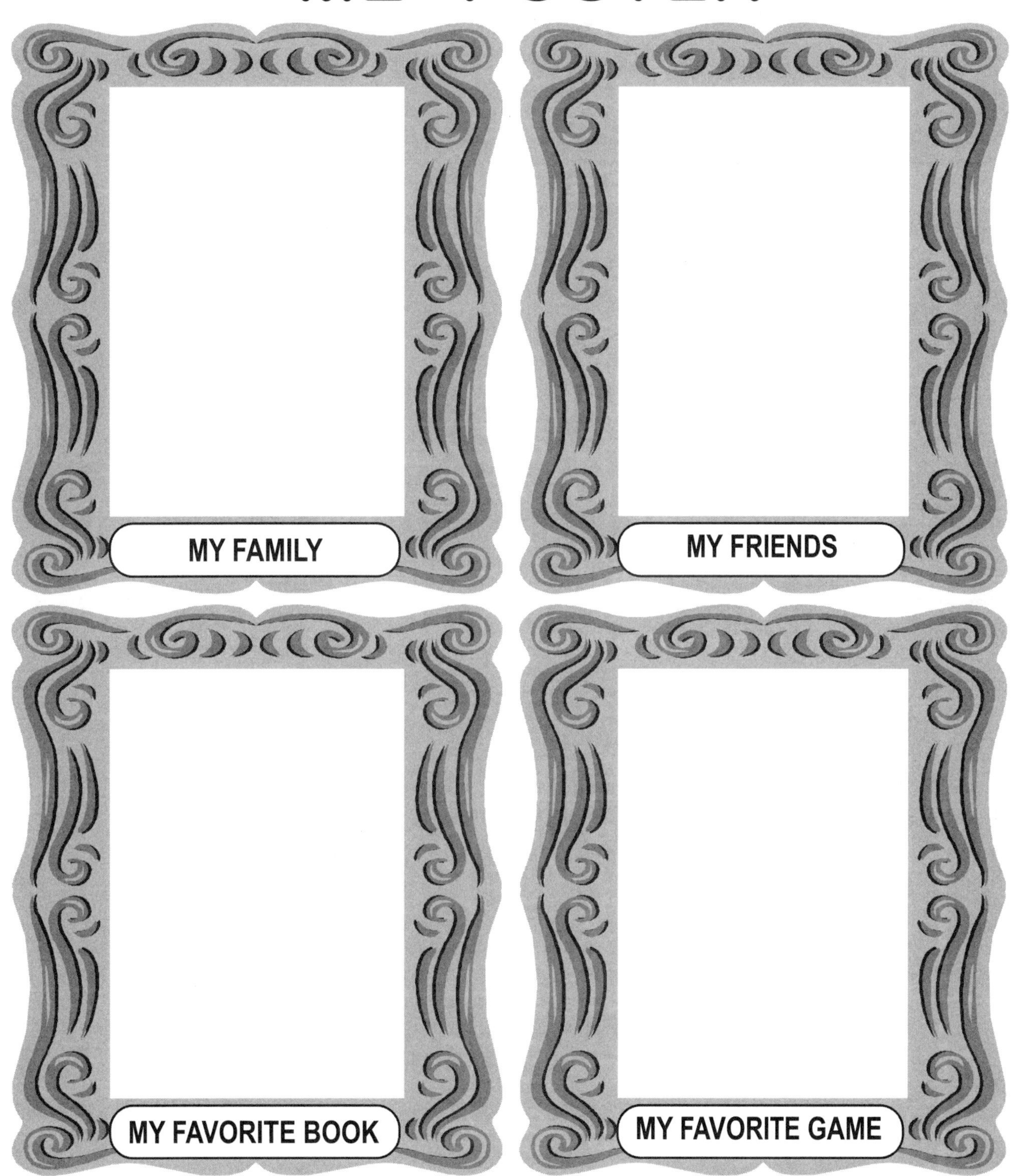

When I grow up, I want to ______________________________

____.

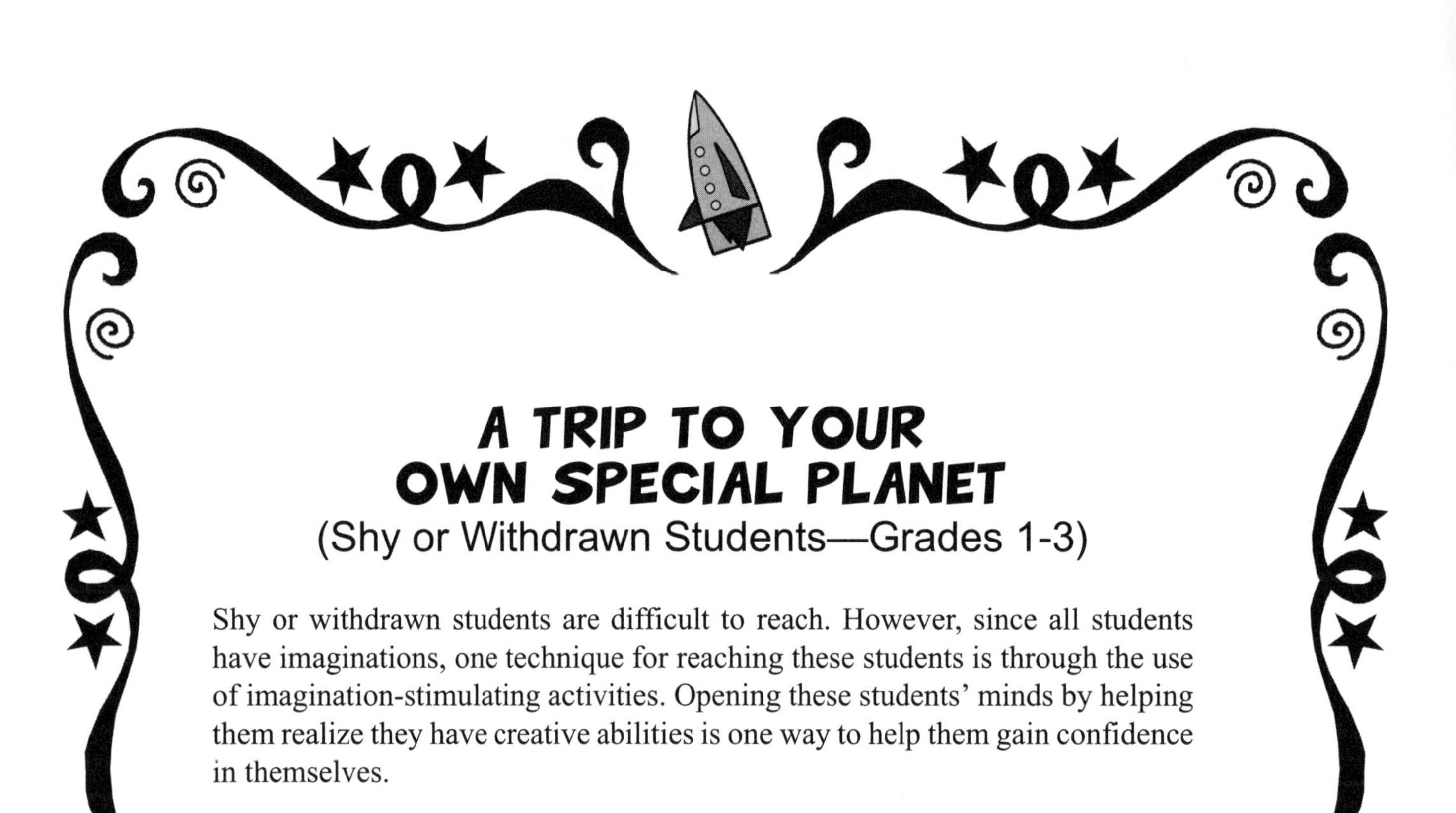

A TRIP TO YOUR OWN SPECIAL PLANET

(Shy or Withdrawn Students—Grades 1-3)

Shy or withdrawn students are difficult to reach. However, since all students have imaginations, one technique for reaching these students is through the use of imagination-stimulating activities. Opening these students' minds by helping them realize they have creative abilities is one way to help them gain confidence in themselves.

This group is designed to help students:

- Develop self-confidence
- Realize their potential abilities

Group candidates:

- Students who do not join in routine activities
- Students who appear to be shy or withdrawn
- Four to six group members from the same or adjoining grade levels

Group preparation:

Interview each student selected individually and explain why the group is forming and how it will work. Then send a parental notification and permission letter (page 209) home with each student selected to be a group member.

Dear ____:

As part of the guidance program, it is my privilege to provide opportunities for students to meet in small groups. The purpose of these groups is to allow the students to acquire information and skills that will help them become more successful in the school setting. School success depends not only on academic ability, but also on self-confidence and social adjustment.

Your child has an opportunity to participate in a group called *A Trip To Your Own Special Planet*. This group is designed to help students who display shyness and withdrawing behaviors to recognize their unique interests, hobbies, and abilities. It is designed to help them develop self-confidence through imagination and creativity.

Each of the eight group meetings will last approximately 30-minutes. The meetings will be held at a time the classroom teacher selects.

Your child knows about the group and has indicated that he or she would like to participate in it. However, no child is ever included in a small-group counseling program without his or her parents' knowledge and permission.

Please indicate, by completing the form below, that you wish to have your child participate in this group or that you do not want him or her to be included.

Return the permission slip to me by ___________________________.

Thank you,

✂- -

☐ I, ____, ***give permission*** for my child to participate in the small-group counseling program for developing self-confidence.

☐ I, ____, ***do not give permission*** for my child to participate in the small-group counseling program for developing self-confidence.

Child's Name ______________________________________ Date ______________

School ______________________________________ Grade ______________

Teacher ______________________________________

Home Phone (_____) _______________ Work Phone (_____) _______________

Parent's Printed Name ______________________________

Parent's Signature ______________________________

Session 1: Shy or Withdrawn Students
INTRODUCTION

Objective:

To introduce the students to the theme of the group and have them make space helmets

Materials Needed:

For each student:
- ☑ Large paper bag
- ☑ Pencil
- ☑ Crayons or markers

For the leader:
- ☑ Scissors

Session Preparation:

Gather the necessary materials.

Session:

- Tell the students that they will meet for eight sessions. During that time, they will plan and take imaginary trips to their own special planets which they have designed and created.
- Distribute a large paper bag, a pencil, and crayons or markers to each student. Tell the students they are to design their own space helmets. Be sure each student draws a space on the helmet that can be cut out so that when the bag is put over his/her head, the student will be able to see out. Tell the students to make their helmets look as authentic as possible.
- As the students make the helmets for their trip to outer space, ask them to think of space names for themselves. They should write these names on their helmets.
- As the students complete their helmets, cut out the space for them to see through.
- Conclude the session by having the students model their helmets and share their space names with the group.
- Collect the helmets and any other materials distributed to the students.

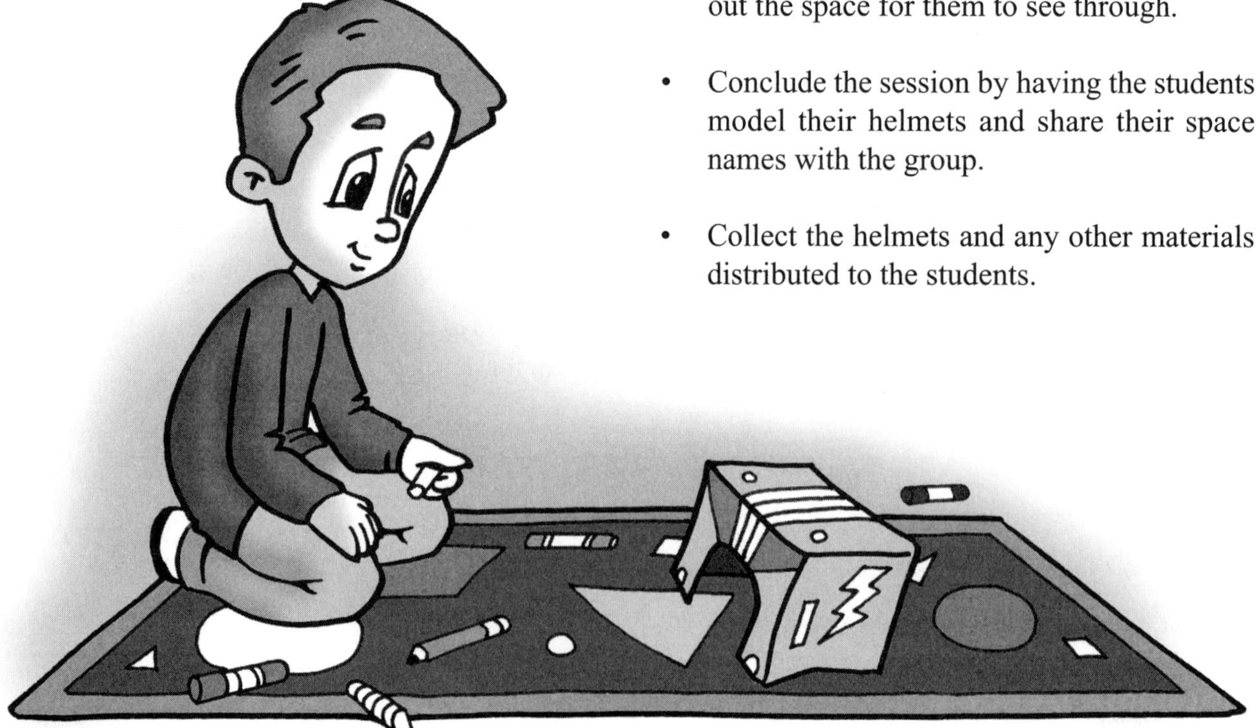

Session 2: Shy or Withdrawn Students
MY PERSONAL SPACESHIP

Objective:

To have the students design a spaceship for their own personal use and show it to the group

Materials Needed:

For each student:
- ☑ 12" x 18" piece of drawing paper
- ☑ Pencil
- ☑ Crayons or markers

For the leader:
- ☑ Tape

Session Preparation:

Gather the necessary materials.

Session:

- Have the students name different modes of transportation to outer space.
- Distribute drawing paper, a pencil, and crayons or markers to each student.
- Have each student design and draw a personal spaceship to travel in on his/her imaginary trip to outer space. Have the students name their spaceships.
- As the students show their spaceships to the group, have them describe where they would sit on their spaceships and what they would do during their journeys to outer space.
- Conclude the session by hanging the drawings around the room.
- Collect any materials that were distributed to the students.

Session 3: Shy or Withdrawn Students
MY PLANET

Objective:

To have the students use their imaginations to visualize traveling through space and describe what they see when they land on their planets

Materials Needed:

For each student:

- ☑ 12" x 18" white drawing paper
- ☑ Pencil
- ☑ Crayons or markers

For the leader:

- ☑ Theme from *Star Wars*™ or similar music
- ☑ CD or tape player
- ☑ Masking tape

Session Preparation:

Gather the necessary materials.

Session:

- As the students enter the room, play the theme from *Star Wars*™ or other music that can create a feeling of outer space. Continue playing the music throughout the session.
- Ask the students to lie on the floor and close their eyes or lower their heads to their desks. Tell them to use their imaginations as they follow your instructions.
- Give the following directions, pausing after each direction for the students to complete each task.

  Imagine you are in your spaceship heading for your own planet in outer space.

  Imagine feeling weightless and floating through space.

  Now you are arriving at your own special planet. You are circling around the planet to see exactly how it looks.

  Circle around your planet several times.

  Land your spaceship on the surface of your planet.

  Get out of your spaceship and look around.

  How do you feel as you look around?

  What do you see? What are the sizes, colors, and shapes of the things you see?

  Open your eyes (Raise your heads).

- Distribute drawing paper, a pencil, and crayons or markers to each student. Have the students draw the way they imagined their planets looked.
- Conclude the session by having the students show their drawings to the group.
- Hang each student's planet drawing next to his/her spaceship picture.
- Collect any materials distributed to the students.

Session 4: Shy or Withdrawn Students
WHAT'S ON MY PLANET

Objective:

To have the students use their imaginations to visualize things on their planet and record their ideas on an activity sheet.

Materials Needed:

For each student:

☑ Copy of *My Own Special Planet* (page 214)
☑ Pencil

For the leader:

☑ Theme from *Star Wars*™ or similar music
☑ CD or Tape player

Session Preparation:

Reproduce *My Own Special Planet* for each student. Gather the other necessary materials.

Session:

- As the students enter the room, play the theme from *Star Wars*™ or other music that can create a feeling of outer space. Continue playing the music throughout the session.
- Ask the students to close their eyes or lower their heads to their desks. Tell them to imagine themselves walking around on their planets. They should be aware of what they see, hear, smell, taste, and touch.
- Have the students open their eyes/raise their heads.
- Distribute *My Own Special Planet* and a pencil to each student. Have them record what they imagined while walking around their planets. (*Note:* If the students are too young to write, the leader should write their answers on their activity sheets.)
- Conclude the lesson by having the students share their activity sheets with the group.

My Own Special Planet

Name ______________________ Planet Name ______________________

Things I See ______________________

____

____

Things I Taste ______________________

____

____

Things I Hear ______________________

____

____

Things I Can Touch ______________________

____

____

Things I Smell ______________________

____

____

On My Planet, I Felt ______________________

____

____

Session 5: Shy or Withdrawn Students
A BUILDING FOR MY PLANET

Objective:

To have the students use their imaginations to design and create a building for their planet

Materials Needed:

For each student:
- ☑ Egg carton
- ☑ Scissors
- ☑ Newspaper
- ☑ Gluestick
- ☑ String
- ☑ Crayons or markers

For the leader:
- ☐ None

Session Preparation:

Gather the necessary materials.

Session:

- Ask the students to think about the previous session. Discuss how they used their five senses as they walked around on their planets.
- Distribute an egg carton, newspaper, string, scissors, a gluestick, and crayons or markers to each student.
- Tell the students to use these materials to design, create, and decorate a building on their planet. They should name their building and know what its purpose is.
- Conclude the lesson by having the students share their buildings, including the building's name and purpose, with the group. Display the buildings in the room and collect any materials distributed to the students.

Session 6: Shy or Withdrawn Students

A SPECTACULAR SIGHT ON MY PLANET

Objective:

To have each student interact more closely with another student in the group

Materials Needed:

For each student:

☑ Piece of drawing paper

For each pair of students:

☑ Crayons or markers

For the leader:

☐ None

Session Preparation:

Gather the necessary materials.

Session:

- Divide the students into pairs. (*Note:* If their is an uneven number of students in the group, the leader should participate.)
- Distribute a piece of paper to each student and crayons or markers to each pair of students.
- Ask the students to imagine one very spectacular thing on their planet. They should visualize the shape and color of what they are imagining.
- Have one partner describe his/her special thing to the other partner, who will draw exactly what is being described. The person describing the special thing may use only words in order to help the other student depict the object on paper.
- Have the partners reverse roles, so each student will have an opportunity to illustrate what his/her partner has described.
- Conclude the session by having each student show and describe his/her picture to the group.

Session 7: Shy or Withdrawn Students

SOMETHING I WOULD BRING BACK TO EARTH FROM MY PLANET

Objective:

To have each student create a memento from his/her planet

Materials Needed:

For each student:

☑ Piece of clay

For the leader:

☐ None

Session Preparation:

Gather the necessary materials.

Session:

- Ask the students to close their eyes or lower their heads to their desks and imagine they are on their own special planets.
- Tell the students to visualize one special thing from their planets that they would like to bring back to Earth to share with the other group members.
- Distribute a piece of clay to each student and tell the students to create whatever they plan to bring back. Tell them to name their mementos.
- Conclude the session by having each student show and describe his/her memento to the group. Collect the clay or allow the students to take their mementos with them.

Session 8: Shy or Withdrawn Students
CONCLUSION

Objective:

To encourage the students to interact with each other

Materials Needed:

For each student:
☐ None

For the leader:
☑ Tape recorder and tape

Session Preparation:

Gather the necessary materials.

Session:

- Ask the students to sit in a circle.
- Put the tape recorder in the middle of the circle.
- Tell the students they are going to take an imaginary trip together. They will create a story about this trip. Each student, in turn, will add one sentence to the story.
- Turn on the tape recorder.
- Going from one student to the next, have each student describe what he/she sees while flying around his/her planet looking for a place to land.
- When each student has contributed a sentence, continue the story in the same manner by having the students describe what they might do or something that might happen while on their planets.
- Continue going around the circle, having each student add a sentence, until the story comes to a normal conclusion.
- Play the tape of the story for the students.
- Conclude the session by asking each group member to state how he/she feels about the group experience.

I'M SPECIAL

(Self-Esteem—Grades K-2)

The importance of positive self-esteem cannot be overemphasized. This trait is essential for all phases of academic and social growth. Students who lack positive self-esteem may not realize their full potential and may be discouraged when interacting with their peers.

This group is designed to help students:

- Recognize their own uniqueness
- Assess their own strengths
- Compare what they think of themselves with what others think of them
- Change negativism through the use of positive activities.

Group candidates:

- Students who show little confidence in their abilities
- Students who depend on the opinions of others to validate their self-worth
- Students who exhibit shyness
- Students who frequently make negative remarks to others
- Students who have difficulty accepting compliments because they do not feel they are worthy of them
- Six to eight students from the same or adjoining grade levels

Group preparation:

Interview each student selected individually and explain why the group is forming and how it will work. Then send a parental notification and permission letter (page 220) home with each student selected to be a group member.

Dear ____:

As part of the guidance program, it is my privilege to provide opportunities for students to meet in small groups. The purpose of these groups is to allow the students to acquire information and skills that will help them become more successful in the school setting. School success depends not only on academic ability, but also on self-confidence and social adjustment.

Your child has the opportunity to participate in a group called *I'm Special*. This group is designed to help students recognize their uniqueness and positive strengths.

Each of the six group meetings will last approximately 30 minutes. The meetings will be held at a time the classroom teacher selects.

Your child knows about the group and has indicated that he or she would like to participate in it. However, no child is ever included in a small-group counseling program without his or her parents' knowledge and permission.

Please indicate, by completing the form below, that you wish to have your child participate in this group or that you do not want him or her to be included.

Return the permission slip to me by ______________________.

Thank you,

✂- -

☐ I, ________________________________, ***give permission*** for my child to participate in the small-group counseling program on self-esteem.

☐ I, ________________________________, ***do not give permission*** for my child to participate in the small-group counseling program on self-esteem.

Child's Name ____________________________ Date ____________

School ____________________________ Grade ____________

Teacher ____________________________

Home Phone (_____) ____________ Work Phone (_____) ____________

Parent's Printed Name ____________________________

Parent's Signature ____________________________

Session 1: Self-Esteem
I'M A SPECIAL PERSON

Objective:

To help the students recognize that each of them is a special person

Materials Needed:

For each student:
- ☑ 3" tagboard circle
- ☑ Crayons or markers
- ☑ Gluestick
- ☑ Scissors

For the leader:
- ☑ Red, yellow, black, and brown yarn
- ☑ Paper punch
- ☑ Scissors

Session Preparation:

Make the tagboard circles. Gather the necessary materials.

Session:

- Introduce the group by telling the students that during their time together, they will learn about themselves and others in the group. It is important for the group members to have fun, but they must to remember that:

  Everyone will have the chance to tell about things and share what he/she has learned.

  No one may say anything unkind about another student.

  When one person is sharing, everyone must listen.

  It is everyone's job to help the others in the group feel good.

- Have each student state his/her first name.
- Give each student an opportunity to be a "star" by standing in front of the group. As each student stands in front of the group, have the other students take turns describing what they see—color of hair, color of eyes, physical build, clothing worn, etc.
- Discuss the fact that each person is unique and special by asking the following questions:

  What did you notice that was different about the students in your group?

  What did you notice that was the same about the students in your group?

  Can you name at least one thing about each person in the group that is special?

- Distribute a tagboard circle and crayons or markers to each student. Have each student to draw a picture his/her face, using the circle as his/her head.
- Give each student yarn that matches the color of his/her hair, scissors, and a gluestick. Tell the students to cut the yarn about the length of their hair, then glue it to the circle.
- Punch a hole in the top of each circle, then thread a long piece of yarn through the hole. Tie the ends together, making a necklace for each of the students to wear.
- Allow the students to take their necklaces with them or collect them and display them in the room. Decide whether to let the students wear the necklaces at each session.
- Collect the distributed materials.

Session 2: Self-Esteem
NAMES ARE SPECIAL

Objective:

To help the students realize their names make them different and special

Materials Needed:

For each student:

- ☑ $8^1/_2$" x 11" piece of tagboard
- ☑ Crayons or markers
- ☑ Gluestick

For the leader:

- ☑ Alphabet noodles or cut-out letters

Session Preparation:

Gather the necessary materials.

Session:

- Begin the group by having the group members state their first, middle, and last name. If they know why they were given their first and/or middle names or after whom they were named have them share this information when they state their names. The leader should go first.
- Distribute a piece of tagboard to each student. Direct the students to fold the tagboard in half so it will stand horizontally.
- Have the students come to the place where the alphabet letters are and find the letters needed to spell their names.
- Distribute crayons or markers and a gluestick to each student.
- Direct the students to glue the letters of their names to the tagboard, then decorate their own special namecards.
- Have the students share their completed namecards.
- Tell the students to look at their namecards and at the other group members' namecards to see what makes theirs special. If necessary, ask questions that will help the students decide what is special about theirs. Suggested questions are:

  Whose name has the most/fewest letters?

  Whose name includes a "W" (or any other letter)?

  Whose name contains the most vowels/consonants?

- Have the students describe ways their namecards can be used.
- Have the students describe what they will do with their namecards.
- Collect any materials that were used.
- Allow the students to take their namecards home with them.

Session 3: Self-Esteem
THINGS I DO WELL

Objective:

To encourage the students think about things they do well

Materials Needed:

For each student:

- ☑ $8^1/_2$" x 11" piece of tagboard
- ☑ Crayons or markers
- ☑ Scissors
- ☑ Metal Hanger
- ☑ String
- ☑ Pencil

For the leader:

- ☑ Hole punch

Session Preparation:

Gather the necessary materials.

Session:

- Tell the students that today's lesson will be about all the different things they can do.
- Recite the following topics and have each student state one or more things that he/she does well in each category:

  Schoolwork
  Sports
  Games
  Chores
  Art
  Music
  Helping Others

- Give each student a hanger, string, crayons, pencil, scissors, and tagboard. Instruct the students to draw, on the tagboard, as many pictures as they wish of things they do well. Tell the students to be careful not put to their pictures too close together and to be sure to leave enough space to draw the first and last initial of their name in block fashion. They should decorate their initials.
- Have the students cut out their pictures and initials.
- Punch a hole in each of the students' pictures and initials.
- Have the students put a string through each hole and attach each picture and initial to the hanger in mobile fashion.
- Have the students share their mobiles. Allow them to take their mobiles home or hang them in the room.
- Collect the distributed materials.

Session 4: Self-Esteem

A COOKIE JAR OF SPECIAL THINGS ABOUT ME

Objective:

To encourage the students to think of special things about themselves

Materials Needed:

For each student:

- ☐ None

For the leader:

- ☑ Cookie jar or container
- ☑ Light brown construction paper
- ☑ Dark brown marker

Session Preparation:

For each person in the group, cut a cookie out of light brown construction paper. Use the brown marker to make chocolate chips. On each cookie, write a statement like:

If I had one wish, I'd wish for_______ .

When I grow up, I'd like to be_______ .

My favorite thing to do is___________ because_______ .

If I could be an animal, I would be a ___________ because_______ .

If I could be someone else, I would like to be ___________ because_______ .

I would like to take a vacation to ___________ because_______ .

One thing I like about myself is ______ .

I am very good at _______ .

Put the cookies in the container.

Session:

- As the students enter the room, have each one take a cookie from the container.
- Have each student, in turn, read and answer the statement on his/her cookie and put the cookie back into the container.
- Mix the cookies and have each student draw a new cookie. Any student who gets the same cookie as before should put it back into the container and draw another.
- Continue this for as long as time allows.

Session 5: Self-Esteem
EVERYONE IS SPECIAL

Objective:

To have the students make positive statements to other group members

Materials Needed:

For each student:
☑ 3" x 5" index card

For the leader:
☑ Marker

Session Preparation:

Write each person's name on a separate index card.

Session:

- Ask the students to make a face that shows how they feel when someone says something unkind to them.
- Ask the students to make a face that shows how they feel when someone says something kind to them.
- Then have the students tell why one face they made showed smiles and the other did not.
- Tell the students that they will be playing a game using cards marked with the names of the group members. You will assign each student a topic and they will make a kind statement about the person whose name is written on the card.
- Shuffle the cards and have each student draw one. The person sitting on the leader's left will go first, then the game will continue on around the circle. After each round, collect the cards, shuffle them, and have each student draw one. If a student draws the same card as drawn in a previous round, have him/her place the card back into the deck and draw another card. Play as many rounds as time allows.
- Suggested topics and examples are:

  Round 1: Something nice about the person's looks.
  Example: Jane's long hair is pretty.

  Round 2: Something the person does well at school.
  Example: Jason is really good at math.

  Round 3: Something about the way the person acts.
  Example: Linda never calls people names.

  Round 4: Something the person does well at recess.
  Example: Clive plays a great game of dodgeball.

  Round 5: Something the person does that is helpful.
  Example: Carlos would loan you a pencil if you didn't have one.

  Round 6: Something the person does in the cafeteria.
  Example: Tamera never cuts into line.

- When the allotted time has elapsed, ask each student to complete the following sentence:

  I felt _________ when I heard something kind said about me.

Session 6: Self-Esteem
OTHER PEOPLE THINK I AM SPECIAL

Objective:

To help the students create memory vests of kind statements for each other

Materials Needed:

For each student:
- ☑ Brown paper grocery bag
- ☑ Crayons or markers
- ☑ Scissors

For the leader:
- ☑ Brown paper grocery bag
- ☑ Scissors

Session Preparation:

Gather the necessary materials.

Session:

- Distribute the brown paper grocery bags to the students. Demonstrate how they should cut the bags. They must first cut the center from the front of the bag, starting at the top and ending at the fold of the bottom. Cut a semicircle from the fold of the bag from the front slit. This will form the opening for the neck and the front of the body. Then cut two holes for the arms. See the illustration below.
- Have the students write their names on their vests.
- Tell the students to use their markers to write one kind thing on each student's vest.
- Have the students put on their vests and model them for the group.
- Thank the students for their cooperation during the group meetings and remind them that each of them has very special qualities.
- Allow the students to take their vests home with them.
- Collect any distributed materials.

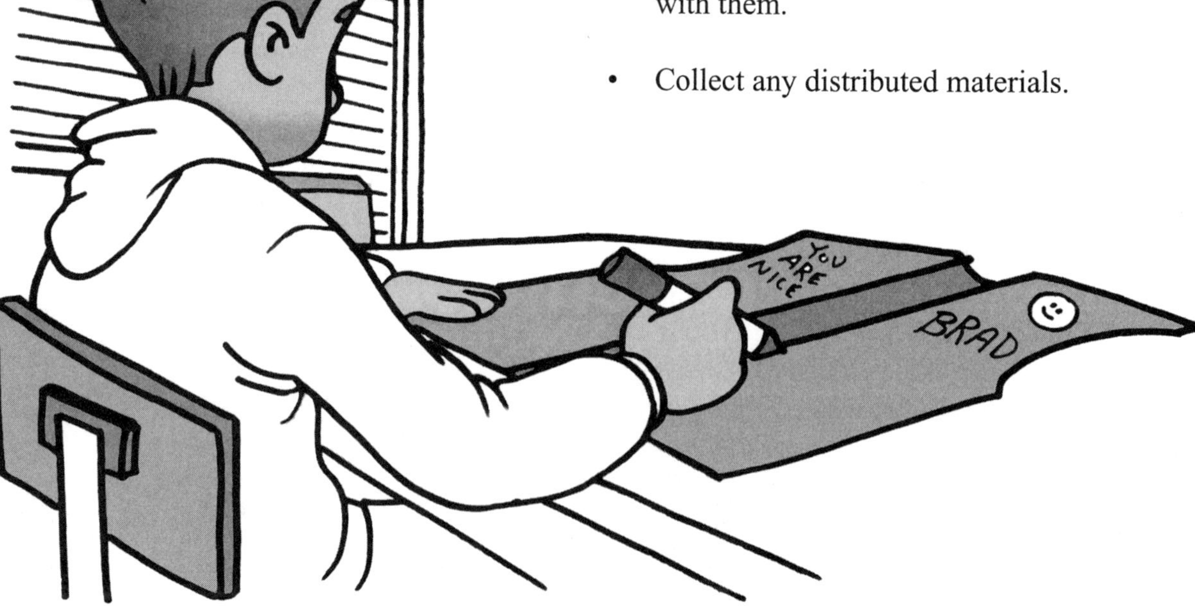

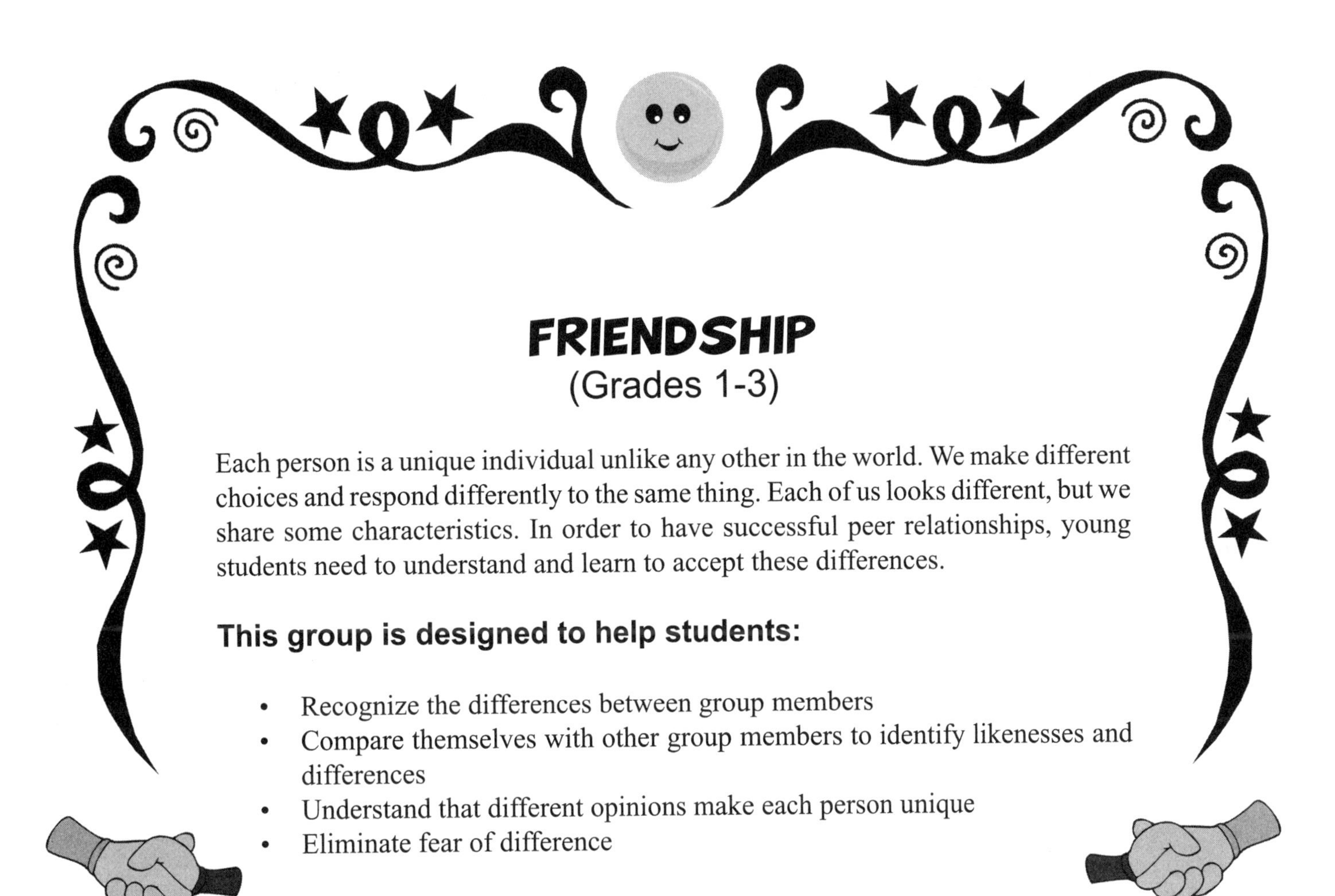

FRIENDSHIP
(Grades 1-3)

Each person is a unique individual unlike any other in the world. We make different choices and respond differently to the same thing. Each of us looks different, but we share some characteristics. In order to have successful peer relationships, young students need to understand and learn to accept these differences.

This group is designed to help students:

- Recognize the differences between group members
- Compare themselves with other group members to identify likenesses and differences
- Understand that different opinions make each person unique
- Eliminate fear of difference

Group candidates:

- Students who are overly self-involved
- Students who lack communication skills
- Students who appear not to accept others as equals
- Six to eight students from the same or adjoining grade levels

Group preparation:

Interview each student selected individually and explain why the group is forming and how it will work. Then send a parental notification and permission letter (page 228) home with each student selected to be a group member.

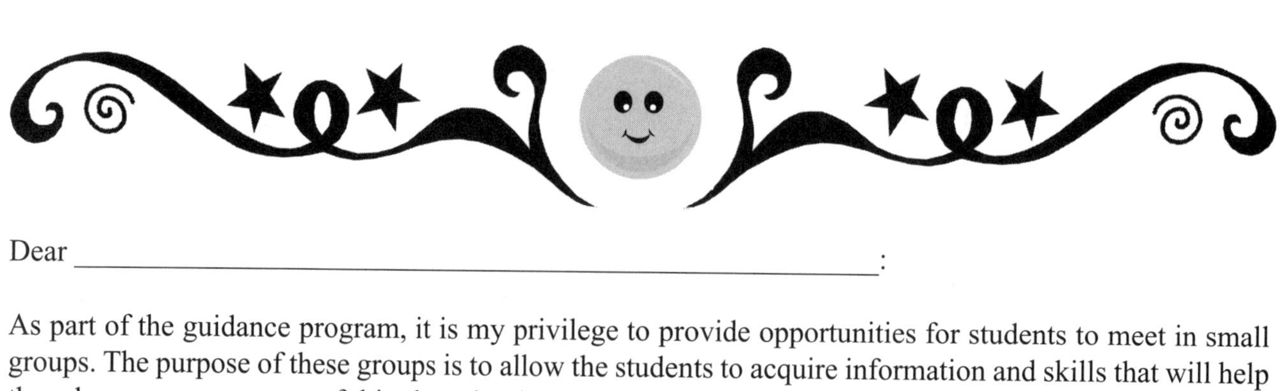

Dear ____:

As part of the guidance program, it is my privilege to provide opportunities for students to meet in small groups. The purpose of these groups is to allow the students to acquire information and skills that will help them become more successful in the school setting. School success depends not only on academic ability, but also on self-confidence and social adjustment.

Your child has an opportunity to participate in a *Friendship* group. This group is designed to help students learn the meaning and responsibilities of friendship. The group will consist of activities that allow group members to become better acquainted with each other and appreciate each others' differences.

Each of the six group meetings will last approximately 30 minutes. The meetings will be held at a time the classroom teacher selects.

Your child knows about the group and has indicated that he or she would like to participate in it. However, no child is ever included in a small-group counseling program without his or her parents' knowledge and permission.

Please indicate, by completing the form below, that you wish to have your child participate in this group or that you do not want him or her to be included.

Return the permission slip to me by _________________________.

Thank you,

✂- -

☐ I, ____________________________________, ***give permission*** for my child to participate in the small-group counseling program on making and keeping friends.

☐ I, ____________________________________, ***do not give permission*** for my child to participate in the small-group counseling program on making and keeping friends.

Child's Name ______________________________ Date ______________

School ______________________________ Grade ______________

Teacher ______________________________

Home Phone (_____) ______________ Work Phone (_____) ______________

Parent's Printed Name ______________________________

Parent's Signature ______________________________

Session 1: Friendship
LOOKS DO NOT TELL THE WHOLE STORY

Objective:

To help the students realize that the way a person looks does not say much about him/her

Materials Needed:

For each student:
- ☑ Copy of *Comparing Looks* (page 230)
- ☑ Pencil

For the leader:
- ☑ Chalkboard and chalk or chart paper and marker

Session Preparation:

Reproduce *Comparing Looks* for each student. Gather the other necessary materials.

Session:

- Introduce the session by having each student state his/her name, grade, and teacher's name. Write each first name on the board. If two students have identical names, write their first name and the first initial of each one's last name.
- Divide the students into pairs.
- Distribute *Comparing Looks* and a pencil to each student. Have the students sit facing each other. Tell the students to look at their partner and answer the questions on the activity sheet down to the word STOP. Explain that if they are not sure how to spell their partner's name, they should refer to the board/chart paper.
- When the students have completed the first section of the activity sheet, tell them they have learned a lot about how their partners look. Then ask:

  By using just the answers on your activity sheet, can you decide whether or not you like your partner? (No.)

- Have the students complete the rest of the activity sheet.
- Allow those students who wish to do so to share one or two things they learned from the activity.
- Collect the activity sheets and save them for the last session. Collect any materials that were distributed.
- Conclude the session by asking each student to complete the following sentences:

  One thing I noticed about the way my partner looked was ____________.

  One thing I could not find out about my partner by looking at him/her was ____________.

COMPARING LOOKS

Name ____________________ Partner's Name ____________________

Look at your partner. Without discussing your answers, write one of your names on each blank.

1. Who has darker hair? ____________________
2. Who has lighter eyes? ____________________
3. Who is shorter? ____________________
4. Who has bigger feet? ____________________
5. Who has darker skin? ____________________
6. Who has more freckles? ____________________
7. Who has longer fingernails? ____________________
8. Who has longer hair? ____________________
9. Describe the clothes your partner is wearing.

____

____

STOP Discuss your answers with your partner.
Do you agree or disagree?

Look at your partner again. Write down three ways you are alike in your looks.

____

____

____

STOP Discuss your answers with your partner.
Do you agree or disagree?

Session 2: Friendship
OUTWARD CHARACTERISTICS

Objective:

To have the students identify the outward characteristics needed to be a friend

Materials Needed:

For each student:

- ☑ Paper bag
- ☑ Pencil
- ☑ Scissors
- ☑ Crayons or markers
- ☑ Gluestick

For the leader:

- ☑ Paper bag
- ☑ Pencil
- ☑ Scissors
- ☑ Crayons or marker
- ☑ Yarn
- ☑ Construction paper

Session Preparation:

Make a sample puppet as shown below. Put the yarn and construction paper where the students can reach them easily. Gather the other necessary materials.

Session:

- Remind the students that the previous lesson's activity showed that just observing a person's looks would not tell them if that person was someone they would want for a friend.
- Distribute a paper bag, pencil, crayons or markers, scissors, and a gluestick to each student. Show the students the sample puppet you made before the session began.
- Explain that the students are to make a puppet similar to yours out of their paper bag. At this time, they are only to make the head. They will add to the puppet after the head is finished. Emphasize they should draw the top lip on the upper fold and the lower lip on the bag so the mouth will be movable.
- When the students are ready to put hair on their puppets, have them select the amount of and color yarn they would like. Then they may return to their desks and glue the yarn to their puppets' heads.
- While the students are making their puppet heads, finish the sample puppet by writing or drawing, on the paper bag body, information that tells about your friends' likes and interests or the likes and interests of someone you might choose for a friend.
- Have the students complete their puppets in the same manner. Tell the students they may glue pieces of construction paper to their puppets to decorate them.
- Ask the students to introduce their puppets to the group.

- Conclude the session by reminding the students that in the previous session they learned that they could not tell whether they liked someone by just looking at him/her. They needed to do something else. Then ask:

  What did you have to do to find out if your puppet would be someone you would like? (Find out more about the puppet's likes and interests.)

  What do you need to do in order to find out whether you would like someone to be your friend? (Find out more about the person's likes and interests.)

- Be sure the students have written their names on their puppets. Collect the puppets and any other materials that were distributed.

Session 3: Friendship

CHARACTERISTICS OF A FRIEND

Objective:

To have the students identify the kind of personality they would like a friend to have, how they would like their friends to treat them, and how they believe they should treat their friends

Materials Needed:

For each student:

- ☑ Puppet from the previous session
- ☑ Pencil

For the leader:

- ☑ Large piece of paper
- ☑ Scissors

Session Preparation:

Cut a large piece of paper into slips the students can write on.

Session:

- Return each student's puppet. Distribute a pencil and two or three slips of paper to each student.
- Ask the students to think about things no one would know about their puppet friends just by looking at them. Examples of these characteristics would be kindness, helpfulness, humorous, etc.
- Have the students write each characteristic on a slip of paper and place the slips of paper inside their puppet paper bag.
- Have the students take the slips from the bag and have each of their puppet friends tell about his/her inner characteristics.
- Discuss how the students would like their puppet friends to treat them and, in turn, how they should treat their friends.
- Identify the characteristics of each puppet that would be helpful in making friends.
- Conclude the session by discussing the characteristics each student might have that could help him/her make and keep friends.
- Collect the puppets and any other distributed materials.

Session 4: Friendship
COMPARING FEELINGS

Objective:

To help the students recognize that friends consider and value of the opinions of others

Materials Needed:

For each student:

- ☑ Copy of *Comparing Feelings* (pages 235-236)
- ☑ Pencil

For the leader:

- ☐ None

Session Preparation:

Reproduce *Comparing Feelings* for each student. Gather the other necessary materials.

Session:

- Introduce the session by telling the students that friends often feel differently about the same thing. One friend may like horseback riding, while another has no desire to get on the back of a horse. These differences are called *opinions,* and it is rare to find two people with exactly the same opinions about everything. Different opinions make us unique.
- Distribute *Comparing Feelings* and a pencil to each student. Have the students complete the activity sheet until they reach the first STOP.
- Have the students compare their answers. As different students share their answers, see if others had the same answers.
- Have the students complete the next two sentences, then STOP.
- Divide the students into groups of three or four. Have each group agree on one thing that makes the group members happy and one thing that makes them sad. The students should record the answers on their activity sheet and finish the sentence by describing how they feel.
- Have each group share its answers.
- Ask the students if they had different opinions when they began the activity. Have them tell how they managed to come to an agreement even though they had different opinions.
- Collect the activity sheets and save them for the last session.
- Conclude the session by telling the students that friends may have different opinions and respecting that others' opinions is one sign of a true friend. Ask each student to complete the following sentence:

  Today I learned that _________ .

COMPARING FEELINGS

Name ______________________________

Complete the following statements with your opinions.

1. My favorite school subject is __________________________ .
2. My favorite food is __________________________ .
3. After school, I like to __________________________ .
4. The clothes I like best are __________________________ .
5. My favorite TV show is __________________________ .
6. The kind of story I most like to read is __________________________ .
7. When I grow up, I want to be __________________________ .
8. My favorite kind of pet is __________________________ .
9. I like to __________________________ .
10. One place I would like to go is __________________________ .

STOP

Compare your answers with those of other students in our group.

Complete the following two sentences:

1. One thing that makes me happy is __________________________

   __________________________ .

2. One thing that makes me sad is __________________________

   __________________________ .

The members of your group must decide on one thing that makes all of you happy and one thing that makes all of you sad. When you have done that, complete the following sentences.

1. One thing that makes everyone in our group happy is_____________

   ____ .

2. One thing that makes everyone in our group sad is _______________

   ____ .

The way I feel about our group's choices is __________________

____ .

Session 5: Friendship
FAMILIES ARE IMPORTANT TO FRIENDS

Objective:

To help the students recognize that everyone's family is different and that it is important to respect how a friends' families will be different from their own

Materials Needed:

For each student:
- ☑ 2 pieces of large drawing paper
- ☑ Pencil
- ☑ Crayons or markers

For the leader:
- ☐ None

Session Preparation:

Gather the necessary materials.

Session:

- Introduce the session by telling the students that one thing that makes them different from others is the kind of family they were born into. Everyone's family is different. Some families have many children, some only one. Some children live with grandparents, aunts or uncles. Some live in foster families or have been adopted. There is no "right" kind of family. Each family is unique, special, and different. This means that friends' families will be different from their own.

- Distribute two large pieces of drawing paper, a pencil, and crayons or markers to each student. On one sheet of paper, have each student draw a picture of the rooms in his/her house or apartment. Then have the students draw their family members in the rooms they might be in at a particular time of the day. (Example: 8:00 p.m.) The family members should be doing what they would usually do at that time of day.

- Have the students choose their favorite holiday and, on a second piece of paper, draw a picture of their home and family that includes the decorations, food eaten, and clothes worn for this holiday.

- Have the students share their drawings with the group. Discuss family similarities and differences.

- Ask the students:

  Do you think your friends' families are different from yours? In what way?

  Do these differences make your family better than your friends' families?

  What is one thing you believe your friends would like about your family?

  What is one thing you like about your friends' families?

- Tell the students that everyone's family is important to him/her. The people in their friends' families mean a lot to their friends. Then ask:

  Would a person who is your friend make unkind remarks about your family?

  Would you be a good friend if you made unkind remarks about your friend's family?

- Then say:

  A true friend respects the feelings of his or her friends and would not say or do anything that would hurt a friend's feelings.

- Collect the drawings and save them for the last session.

- Conclude the session by asking each student to complete the following sentences:

  Today I learned that my family is special because_________.

  One thing I learned about another group member's family was_________.

  I also learned that a true friend will not _________ about a friend's family.

Session 6: Friendship
CONCLUSION

Objective:

To summarize the concepts presented in the group

Materials Needed:

For each student:
- ☑ Pencil
- ☑ Crayons or markers

For the leader:
- ☑ Marker
- ☑ 7 or more pieces of tagboard

Session Preparation:

Write one very large letter from the word FRIENDS on each piece of tagboard. If there are more than seven students in the group, make duplicate letters. Gather the necessary other materials.

Session:

- Review the concepts presented in previous group sessions:
  - Outward appearances do not tell the whole story
  - Outward characteristics are important
  - Characteristics of a friend
  - Acceptance of the opinions of friends
  - Respect for a friend's family.
- Distribute one piece of tagboard, a pencil, and crayons or markers to each student. Depending on the size of the group, some students may have two letters.
- Tell each student to use his/her letter to tell something about what he/she has learned in group. For example, if one of the letters was *B* the student may decide to say that "Being a friend is being respectful of a friend's feelings."
- Tell the students that once they have decided what they are going to say, they may design a poster by decorating their tagboard letter.
- Have the students share their sayings with the group.
- Tell the students to fold their posters in half and use them as a cover for their papers. Return all the students' papers and have them put them into their folders.
- Collect any distributed materials.
- Conclude the group by thanking the students for their participation. As leader, finish by going around the group and completing the following sentence for each group member.

  I know you will be a good friend because you_________.

ABOUT THE AUTHOR

Arden Martenz is the president of Mar*co Products. She is the author/coauthor of more that 30 books relating to the field of guidance. She was an elementary teacher in grades three and five, an elementary counselor for 19 years, and a graduate instructor for classroom management in Pennsylvania.

A graduate of the University of Washington in Seattle, Washington and a holder of a Master's Degree in guidance and counseling from Lehigh University in Pennsylvania, she now spends her time creating materials for guidance counselors and presenting workshops throughout the country. In the year 2000, she was named an outstanding educator in Bucks County for the previous century.

She is married, has two sons and a daughter, and six grandchildren.